A Choice of Swinburne's Verse

by Robert Nye

A Choice of
SWINBURNE'S
Verse

Selected

with an introduction by

ROBERT NYE

FABER AND FABER

3 Queen Square

London

First published in 1973
by Faber and Faber Limited
3 Queen Square London WC1
Printed in Great Britain by
Latimer Trend & Company Ltd Plymouth
All rights reserved

ISBN 0 571 09261 6 (paper covered edition)
ISBN 0 571 09260 8 (hard bound edition)

Contents

Editor's Note

Most of the poems in this volume of selections are drawn from the first series of *Poems and Ballads* (1866), simply because in my opinion that book represents Swinburne at the height of his powers. I was unable to work with the original edition, published by John Camden Hotten, but used the Chatto and Windus edition of 1894. For the text of *Atalanta in Calydon* (first published in 1865 by Edward Moxon), and the remaining poems, I used the twenty-volume Bonchurch Edition of *The Complete Works of Algernon Charles Swinburne*, edited by Sir Edmund Gosse and Thomas J. Wise (1925-7), published by William Heinemann. It should be noted that Wise's reputation does not encourage faith in the accuracy of the Bonchurch Swinburne, and that it is in any case certainly not complete. The text of stanzas VII and IX of the translation of Villon's *La Belle Heaulmyère*, censored in all Victorian editions, has been restored from the original manuscript (BM Ashley MS 5071). Swinburne's holograph supplies several alternative readings, and is apparently a draft which he revised when preparing the poem for publication in *Poems and Ballads: Second Series* (1878). Unlike Wise, I have chosen the words which exactly match the number of asterisks in the early editions.

The interested reader may also care to consult Cecil Y. Lang's six-volume edition of *The Swinburne Letters* (1959-62), published by the Yale University Press; Harold Nicolson's *Swinburne* (1926), published by Macmillan; Georges Lafourcade's *La Jeunesse de Swinburne* (1928), published by the Oxford University Press; and Edmund

Wilson's edition of Swinburne's two novels *Love's Cross-Currents* and *Lesbia Brandon* (1962), published by Farrar, Straus and Cudahy.

To Karl M. Abenheimer

The creative process has a feminine quality, and the creative work arises from unconscious depths—we might truly say from the realm of the Mothers. Whenever the creative force predominates, life is ruled and shaped by the unconscious rather than by the conscious will, and the ego is swept along on an underground current, becoming nothing more than a helpless observer of events. The progress of the work becomes the poet's fate and determines his psychology. It is not Goethe that creates *Faust*, but *Faust* that creates Goethe.

C. G. Jung, *Collected Works,*
Vol. 15: The Spirit in Man,
Art and Literature

Introduction

Swinburne's reputation as an empty vessel making a lot of meaningless if musical noise relates to only about nine-tenths of his poetic production. The other tenth is worth salvaging. The difficulty of the operation lies in the fact that it is not, as it were, a constant tenth. Each reader will have his own necessary Swinburne which, if he would begin to understand the man's peculiar contribution to English verse, he should discover. That is what I have tried to do in assembling this volume of selections. My starting-point, apart from personal taste, lay in some observations of T. S. Eliot's:

> It is a question of some nicety to decide how much must be read of any particular poet. And it is not a question merely of the size of the poet. There are some poets whose every line has unique value. There are others who can be taken by a few poems universally agreed upon. There are others who need be read only in selections, but what selections are read will not very much matter. Of Swinburne, we should like to have the *Atalanta* entire, and a volume of selections which should certainly contain *The Leper, Laus Veneris,* and *The Triumph of Time.* It ought to contain many more, but there is perhaps no other single poem which it would be an error to omit.*

* *The Sacred Wood* (1920). It was the present editor's intention to fulfil Eliot's wish and include the *Atalanta* entire, but the format of the series to which this volume belongs has allowed for the choruses only.

Eliot's paper on Swinburne appears to me almost wholly cogent, and helpful for a modern reader to bear in mind, not least because it raises a number of objections to Swinburne most commonly made, and deals with each one seriously. There is the question of 'diffuseness', for example, which Eliot counters by declaring that had Swinburne practised greater concentration his verse would be 'not better in the same kind, but a different thing':

His diffuseness is one of his glories. That so little material as appears to be employed in *The Triumph of Time* should release such an amazing number of words, requires what there is no reason to call anything but genius. You could not condense *The Triumph of Time*. You could only leave out. And this would destroy the poem; though no one stanza seems essential. Similarly, a considerable quantity—a volume of selections—is necessary to give the quality of Swinburne although there is perhaps no one poem essential in this selection.

Then again, there are the complaints of the first Victorian critics to be considered. It will be remembered that they professed themselves morally repulsed. John Morley's unsigned attack in the *Saturday Review* on *Poems and Ballads* (1866) may be quoted as typical:

It is of no use to scold Mr Swinburne for grovelling down among the nameless shameless abominations which inspire him with such frenzied delight. They excite his imagination to its most vigorous efforts, they seem to him the themes most proper for poetic treatment, and they suggest ideas which, in his opinion, it is highly to be wished that English men and women should brood upon and make their own. He finds that these fleshly things are his strong part, so he sticks to them. Is it wonderful that he should? And at all events he deserves credit for the audacious courage with which he has revealed to the world a mind all aflame with the feverish carnality of a schoolboy over the dirtiest passages in Lemprière. It is not every poet who would ask us all go hear him tuning his lyre in a stye.

This at least concedes, even if ironically, that a degree of feverishness was vital to Swinburne. Others detected no merit at all in what they regarded as the rankest self-indulgence. Robert Buchanan, in the *Athenaeum*, again anonymously, likened Swinburne to Petronius's Gito, 'seated in the tub of Diogenes, conscious of the filth and whining at the stars'. Many of these early critics could see no farther than what looked to them like blasphemy and obscenity. At the height of the critical attack *Punch* announced that the poet should change his name to what was evidently its true form: SWINE-BORN. More literate and good-humoured judges still found him sensational and monotonous, all heat, voluptuous, pagan, out to shock. Eliot in the paper already cited from *The Sacred Wood* will have none of this. His refusal to condemn Swinburne on moral grounds may at first sight appear merely ingenious, but examined I think it can be shown to be the exercise of a discrimination in the service of a seriousness sufficiently deep as to be unshockable. 'The poetry is not morbid, it is not erotic, it is not destructive. These are adjectives which can be applied to the material, the human feelings, which in Swinburne's case do not exist. *The morbidity is not of human feeling but of language.*' (My italics.) This is precise, and presents us with a critical point from which it is possible to view an unpopular poet without prejudice.

The sea, regret, kissing, delirium, fire, weariness, roses,

[15]

pain, cliffs, loss, stars, downs, the sun, wine, thunder, blood, pleasure, death, swallows in the foam, Mary Queen of Scots, the wind—Swinburne's range of reference as revealed through imagery and subject-matter is not wide, and scarcely need detain us from the more interesting and complicated business of his language, what Browning called his 'fuzz of words'. If we seek for one thing which his poems have in common it will be found to be their literariness. His imagination was imitative, it fed on books, it feasted on other men's wits. I do not think that there is anything especially inferior in this. A poet finds his inspiration where he can. For reasons which lie beyond the reach of these notes, Swinburne did not lead a life full of events. At a certain point his capacity to respond to direct experience seems to have been arrested. Harold Nicolson, discussing this phenomenon and Swinburne's curious 'imperviousness to impressions', observes that:

It is a daring but not untenable paradox to contend that Swinburne's emotional receptivity began to ossify in 1857, that is, in his twenty-first year. The experiences which he had by then absorbed became his future attitudes: all subsequent experiences were little more than superficial acceptances or, as his passion for babies, special kinds of belief.*

Nicolson goes on to notice that when Swinburne writes of the sea, as he usually does, and of storms at sea, which is more often than not in the next breath, it is almost invariably with reference to a specific storm which he experienced between Dover and Ostend *when he was eighteen,* and he infers that 'such imperviousness discloses a nervous system of surpassing eccentricity'. Swinburne's nervous system is unfortunately not altogether beside the

* *Swinburne* (1926).

point, but I prefer to confine my remarks to his verses. It is here to be observed how many of these derive from what he picked up in the way of education at Eton and Balliol, or from his later and perhaps more comprehensive contact with works of scholarship. *A Ballad of Life* and *A Ballad of Death,* for example, could hardly have been constructed without knowledge of the models of *canzoni* by Dante and Cavalcanti which he would have studied in D. G. Rossetti's *The Early Italian Poets* (1861); *In the Orchard* and *A Ballad of Burdens* derive from the antique French; *The Masque of Queen Bersabe* is a skilful copy of one kind of medieval miracle play; *After Death* and *A Lyke-wake Song* are imitations of Border Ballads; the influence of the antiphonal rhythms of the Psalms and the imagery of the Old Testament generally is everywhere to be felt; the *Atalanta,* most ambitious of all, is an attempt to accommodate and re-create in English verse the spirit, as well as the form, and even to a limited extent the metres, of Greek poetry—astonishing alike in its faculty of imitation and its fidelity to Attic principles, however cleverly infused these latter become with obsessions proper to Swinburne alone. The *Atalanta* might be criticized as exceptional in its success, for even those who most dislike what Swinburne was trying to do will frequently concede that he achieved a kind of grandeur in its choruses, sustaining the tone throughout and combining classicism and modernity in a manner that will bear comparison with Shelley's *Prometheus Unbound.* What is truly remarkable about the *Atalanta,* however, is that it is not so much an isolated peak as the summit of a whole range of imitative exercises of a similar type, and what is remarkable about these exercises is that they are really more often than not good poems. We do not expect pastiche to be good poetry, our twentieth-century opinions about the function of personality tell us that pastiche is unlikely ever to be poetry at all, but in Swinburne it is. This may have come about because books were in certain essential respects more real to him than persons. He could write poems immediately inspired by a form, or out of love of technique for its own sake. All he needs is the ghost, the authority. It is a pity he did not turn his hand more often to translation, for when he did the result was a simplicity not otherwise to be found in him. 'Swinburne's Villon is not Villon very exactly, but it is perhaps the best Swinburne we have.'* Even when Swinburne is not translating he very often in his finest verse gives us the impression that he must be. Anapaests and dactyls do not ride altogether comfortably in the English language, but it is not just a matter of foreign accents. The ghost, the authority, the illusion of another poem beyond the shape of the one we are reading, supplying its imperfections, filling in its vacuities, giving it some overpowering sanction—this is pervasive in any attentive reading of Swinburne. And at the same time we remember that his muse is actually supersaturated in other men's music: Catullus, Sophocles, Aeschylus, Aristophanes, his beloved Elizabethans, the courtly poets and the troubadours. And, of women, always and only Sappho. The upshot is literary poetry, but literary poetry of a high and passionate kind. Its world is Swinburne's own, and self-complete.

There is, though, even when the force and flexibility of his versification has been taken into account, the unpleasant feeling that we are getting something at second-hand. Nicolson skates over this too fast by claiming that the feelings provoked in Swinburne by a work of art were just as direct, as real, and as original, as the feelings provoked in Wordsworth by the contemplation of nature. But that ignores or denies the effect of the existing *sensi-*

* Ezra Pound, *How to Read* (1931).

[18]

bility in Swinburne's sources of inspiration. If Swinburne himself had not had this to contend with, it is probable that he would have been less chronically given to embellishment. You cannot decorate your impressions of a hill or a flower beyond a certain point without appearing to yourself as fanciful and silly, but if your impulse lies in someone else's impressions then you may very well go on about the quarrel of decoration, the exquisite task of ornament and amplification, for fifty-five stanzas, all in the one hypnotic measure, just in order to stake your claim to the subject and convince yourself of its justice. The elegance of Swinburne's prosody—and his classical experiments in particular seem to me of conspicuous interest—should not deafen us to the fact that his poems are sometimes distressingly inconclusive. They do not end, they only stop. He tends to *use* his themes as what Eliot calls 'the merest point of diffusion'. The drift of this, in content as well as in what the treatment of the content implies, could be defined as deathwards. Satisfaction in this verse is always withheld; the poet remains unsatisfied; surfeit being impossible, happiness is made akin to an interminable death-agony. Why? Cecil Y. Lang, who otherwise seems to me to overvalue Swinburne in introducing his edition of *The Swinburne Letters* (1959–62), performs a service by referring us back to an observation of Maud Bodkin's:

By the neurotic, medical psychologists tell us, death is envisaged, not objectively, as 'normal people' are expected to view it—as the end of life, an event with social, moral and legal implications—but as 'a quiescent resolution of affective excitement'; 'the tendency to it is an effort of the organism to restore the quiescent equilibrium', realized once (it is supposed) at the beginning of life, within the mother's womb. Like the neurotic, the poet or his reader, dreaming on the river that breaks at last into the free ocean, sees in this image his own life and death, not at all in their social and legal implications, but in accordance with a deep organic need for release from conflict and tension.*

This reads somewhat naïvely perhaps, and Miss Bodkin's opinion of death as something 'with social, moral and legal implications' may be felt to by no means exhaust the possibilities of that event even for 'normal people'. She is actually discussing a poem by Matthew Arnold; all the same, the relevance of this passage to a great deal of Swinburne will be obvious, especially to that distinctive kind of maternal-eternal confusion which reaches its climax in *The Triumph of Time*.

Finally it is the words we have to notice. We cannot miss them. There are so many, and they are so frequently mechanical, blurred, or inaccurate. 'The rhythm-building faculty was in Swinburne, and was perhaps the chief part of his genius. The word-selecting, word-castigating faculty was nearly absent.' Thus Pound, who perceives also that Swinburne 'neglected the value of words as words, and was intent on their value as sounds', while acknowledging that 'no one else has made such music in English' and that it is 'a music which will compare with Chaucer's *Hide Absalon thi gilte tresses clere* or with any other maker you like'. Why there is a species of word-disease in Swinburne, and what that disease signifies for other poets, these are harder questions, but ones which Eliot comes near enough to answering when he says, 'Language in a healthy state presents the object, is so close to the object that the two are identified,' and then goes on:

They are identified in the verse of Swinburne solely

* *Archetypal Patterns in Poetry* (1934).

[20]

because the object has ceased to exist, because the meaning is merely the hallucination of meaning, because language, uprooted, has adapted itself to an independent life of atmospheric nourishment. In Swinburne, for example, we see the word 'weary' flourishing in this way independent of the particular and actual weariness of flesh or spirit. The bad poet dwells partly in a world of objects and partly in a world of words, and he never can get them to fit. Only a man of genius could dwell so exclusively and consistently among words as Swinburne. His language is not, like the language of bad poetry, dead. It is very much alive, with this singular life of its own.

The truth of this now appears to me as self-demonstrated in the verses, accounting for their fervour and vitality, their sometimes prismatic diction, as well as less agreeable things, such as their slippery alliterativeness and their 'music' which is often just so much multiplication of the cells of sound. It has not always been so clear. I once set out to write a life of Swinburne and only gave up the enterprise when it came home to me that he had hardly had one. What little living the man ever managed was in language, in these intricate rhapsodic excursions, these high-pitched incantatory poems where words breed and feed upon themselves, metaphor runs riot and takes the place of thought, allusion tries to do the job of feeling, and it is seldom that any lasting total impression is left upon the reader's mind other than a sense of the poet's own excitement at the time of writing. That is indelible enough, and as sheer lyric vehemence produces oddnesses of its own, a surprising life and liveliness, not necessarily delusive or false, delighting in emotion no less than in the movements of the mind, yet not at all erotic or, even where beginning in Eros, as in Sappho's passion for Anactoria, eventually going somewhere else. Swinburne

[21]

lived in language, but in a peculiar state of fever where one word would do as well as another, so long as the strophe was not spoiled, and the general music was the same. The poems are a kind of dance of death, the more grotesque for being a St. Vitus's Dance. But then again there are the unanswerable moments, the pauses, the perfect lines which give the lie to all that one can say, and prove the man a poet, as in *Laus Veneris*

> *Knights gather, riding sharp for cold; I know*
> *The ways and woods are strangled with the snow*

or, in *In the Orchard*

> *The grass is thick and cool, it lets us lie.*
> *Kissed upon either cheek and either eye,*
> *I turn to thee as some green afternoon*
> *Turns toward sunset, and is loth to die;*
> *Ah God, ah God that day should be so soon.*

or, in *The Leper*

> *Nothing is better, I well know*
> *Than love; no amber in cold sea*
> *Or gathered berries under snow:*
> *That is well seen of her and me.*

or, in *Before Parting*

> *I know not how this last month leaves your hair*
> *Less full of purple colour and hid spice,*
> *And that luxurious trouble of closed eyes*
> *Is mixed with meaner shadow and waste care;*
> *And love, kissed out by pleasure, seems not yet*
> *Worth patience to regret.*

or *The Sundew*, which I shall quote in full for those who have read this far but may now be unlikely to read much further without it:

A little marsh-plant, yellow green,
And pricked at lip with tender red.
Tread close, and either way you tread
Some faint black water jets between
Lest you should bruise the curious head.

A live thing maybe; who shall know?
The summer knows and suffers it;
For the cool moss is thick and sweet
Each side, and saves the blossom so
That it lives out the long June heat.

The deep scent of the heather burns
About it; breathless though it be,
Bow down and worship; more than we
Is the least flower whose life returns,
Least weed renascent in the sea.

We are vexed and cumbered in earth's sight
With wants, with many memories;
These see their mother what she is,
Glad-growing, till August leave more bright
The apple-coloured cranberries.

Wind blows and bleaches the strong grass,
Blown all one way to shelter it
From trample of strayed kine, with feet
Felt heavier than the moorhen was,
Strayed up past patches of wild wheat.

You call it sundew: how it grows,
If with its colour it have breath,
If life taste sweet to it, if death
Pain its soft petal, no man knows:
Man has no sight or sense that saith.

My sundew, grown of gentle days,
In these green miles the spring begun
Thy growth ere April had half done
With the soft secret of her ways
Or June made ready for the sun.

O red-lipped mouth of marsh-flower,
I have a secret halved with thee.
The name that is love's name to me
Thou knowest, and the face of her
Who is my festival to see.

The hard sun, as thy petals knew,
Coloured the heavy moss-water:
Thou wert not worth green midsummer
Nor fit to live to August blue,
O sundew, not remembering her.

ROBERT NYE

Edinburgh
February 1972

A Ballad of Life

I found in dreams a place of wind and flowers,
    Full of sweet trees and colour of glad grass,
    In midst whereof there was
A lady clothed like summer with sweet hours.
Her beauty, fervent as a fiery moon,
    Made my blood burn and swoon
        Like a flame rained upon.
Sorrow had filled her shaken eyelids' blue,
And her mouth's sad red heavy rose all through
        Seemed sad with glad things gone.

She held a little cithern by the strings,
    Shaped heartwise, strung with subtle-coloured hair
    Of some dead lute-player
That in dead years had done delicious things.
The seven strings were named accordingly;
    The first string charity,
        The second tenderness,
The rest were pleasure, sorrow, sleep, and sin,
And loving-kindness, that is pity's kin
        And is most pitiless.

There were three men with her, each garmented
    With gold and shod with gold upon the feet;
    And with plucked ears of wheat
The first man's hair was wound upon his head:
His face was red, and his mouth curled and sad;
    All his gold garment had
        Pale stains of dust and rust.

A riven hood was pulled across his eyes;
The token of him being upon this wise
    Made for a sign of Lust.

The next was Shame, with hollow heavy face
  Coloured like green wood when flame kindles it.
  He hath such feeble feet
They may not well endure in any place.
His face was full of grey old miseries,
  And all his blood's increase
    Was even increase of pain.
The last was Fear, that is akin to Death;
He is Shame's friend, and always as Shame saith
    Fear answers him again.

My soul said in me; This is marvellous,
  Seeing the air's face is not so delicate
  Nor the sun's grace so great,
If sin and she be kin or amorous.
And seeing where maidens served her on their knees,
  I bade one crave of these
    To know the cause thereof.
Then Fear said: I am Pity that was dead.
And Shame said: I am Sorrow comforted.
    And Lust said: I am Love.

Thereat her hands began a lute-playing
  And her sweet mouth a song in a strange tongue;
  And all the while she sung
There was no sound but long tears following
Long tears upon men's faces, waxen white
  With extreme sad delight.
    But those three following men
Became as men raised up among the dead;
Great glad mouths open and fair cheeks made red
    With child's blood come again.

Then I said: Now assuredly I see
  My lady is perfect, and transfigureth
  All sin and sorrow and death,
Making them fair as her own eyelids be,
Or lips wherein my whole soul's life abides;
  Or as her sweet white sides
    And bosom carved to kiss.
Now therefore, if her pity further me,
Doubtless for her sake all my days shall be
    As righteous as she is.

Forth, ballad, and take roses in both arms,
  Even till the top rose touch thee in the throat
Where the least thornprick harms;
  And girdled in thy golden singing-coat,
Come thou before my lady and say this;
  Borgia, thy gold hair's colour burns in me,
    Thy mouth makes beat my blood in feverish rhymes;
  Therefore so many as these roses be,
    Kiss me so many times.
Then it may be, seeing how sweet she is,
  That she will stoop herself none otherwise
    Than a blown vine-branch doth,
  And kiss thee with soft laughter on thine eyes,
    Ballad, and on thy mouth.

A Ballad of Death

Kneel down, fair Love, and fill thyself with tears,
Girdle thyself with sighing for a girth
Upon the sides of mirth,
Cover thy lips and eyelids, let thine ears
Be filled with rumour of people sorrowing;
Make thee soft raiment out of woven sighs
Upon the flesh to cleave,
Set pains therein and many a grievous thing,
And many sorrows after each his wise
For armlet and for gorget and for sleeve.

O Love's lute heard about the lands of death,
Left hanged upon the trees that were therein;
O Love and Time and Sin,
Three singing mouths that mourn now underbreath,
Three lovers, each one evil spoken of;
O smitten lips wherethrough this voice of mine
Came softer with her praise;
Abide a little for our lady's love.
The kisses of her mouth were more than wine,
And more than peace the passage of her days.

O Love, thou knowest if she were good to see.
O Time, thou shalt not find in any land
Till, cast out of thine hand,
The sunlight and the moonlight fail from thee,
Another woman fashioned like as this.
O Sin, thou knowest that all thy shame in her
Was made a goodly thing;

Yea, she caught Shame and shamed him with her kiss,
With her fair kiss, and lips much lovelier
Than lips of amorous roses in late spring.

By night there stood over against my bed
Queen Venus with a hood striped gold and black,
Both sides drawn fully back
From brows wherein the sad blood failed of red,
And temples drained of purple and full of death.
Her curled hair had the wave of sea-water
And the sea's gold in it.
Her eyes were as a dove's that sickeneth.
Strewn dust of gold she had shed over her,
And pearl and purple and amber on her feet.

Upon her raiment of dyed sendaline
Were painted all the secret ways of love
And covered things thereof,
That hold delight as grape-flowers hold their wine;
Red mouths of maidens and red feet of doves,
And brides that kept within the bride-chamber
Their garment of soft shame,
And weeping faces of the wearied loves
That swoon in sleep and awake wearier,
With heat of lips and hair shed out like flame.

The tears that through her eyelids fell on me
Made mine own bitter where they ran between
As blood had fallen therein,
She saying; Arise, lift up thine eyes and see
If any glad thing be or any good
Now the best thing is taken forth of us;
Even she to whom all praise
Was as one flower in a great multitude,
One glorious flower of many and glorious,
One day found gracious among many days:

Even she whose handmaiden was Love—to whom
At kissing times across her stateliest bed
Kings bowed themselves and shed
Pale wine, and honey with the honeycomb,
And spikenard bruised for a burnt-offering;
Even she between whose lips the kiss became
As fire and frankincense;
Whose hair was as gold raiment on a king,
Whose eyes were as the morning purged with flame,
Whose eyelids as sweet savour issuing thence.

Then I beheld, and lo on the other side
My lady's likeness crowned and robed and dead.
Sweet still, but now not red,
Was the shut mouth whereby men lived and died.
And sweet, but emptied of the blood's blue shade,
The great curled eyelids that withheld her eyes.
And sweet, but like spoilt gold,
The weight of colour in her tresses weighed.
And sweet, but as a vesture with new dyes,
The body that was clothed with love of old.

Ah! that my tears filled all her woven hair
And all the hollow bosom of her gown—
Ah! that my tears ran down
Even to the place where many kisses were,
Even where her parted breast-flowers have place,
Even where they are cloven apart—who knows not this?
Ah! the flowers cleave apart
And their sweet fills the tender interspace;
Ah! the leaves grown thereof were things to kiss
Ere their fine gold was tarnished at the heart.

Ah! in the days when God did good to me,
Each part about her was a righteous thing;

Her mouth an almsgiving,
The glory of her garments charity,
The beauty of her bosom a good deed,
In the good days when God kept sight of us;
Love lay upon her eyes,
And on that hair whereof the world takes heed;
And all her body was more virtuous
Than souls of women fashioned otherwise.

Now, ballad, gather poppies in thine hands
And sheaves of brier and many rusted sheaves
Rain-rotten in rank lands,
Waste marigold and late unhappy leaves
And grass that fades ere any of it be mown;
And when thy bosom is filled full thereof
Seek out Death's face ere the light altereth,
And say 'My master that was thrall to Love
Is become thrall to Death.'
Bow down before him, ballad, sigh and groan,
But make no sojourn in thy outgoing;
For haply it may be
That when thy feet return at evening
Death shall come in with thee.

Laus Veneris

Asleep or waking is it? for her neck,
Kissed over close, wears yet a purple speck
   Wherein the pained blood falters and goes out,
Soft, and stung softly—fairer for a fleck.

But though my lips shut sucking on the place,
There is no vein at work upon her face;
   Her eyelids are so peaceable, no doubt
Deep sleep has warmed her blood through all its ways.

Lo, this is she that was the world's delight;
The old grey years were parcels of her might;
   The strewings of the ways wherein she trod
Were the twain seasons of the day and night.

Lo, she was thus when her clear limbs enticed
All lips that now grow sad with kissing Christ,
   Stained with blood fallen from the feet of God,
The feet and hands whereat our souls were priced.

Alas, Lord, surely thou art great and fair.
But lo her wonderfully woven hair!
   And thou didst heal us with thy piteous kiss;
But see now, Lord; her mouth is lovelier.

She is right fair; what hath she done to thee?
Nay, fair Lord Christ, lift up thine eyes and see;
   Had now thy mother such a lip—like this?
Thou knowest how sweet a thing it is to me.

Inside the Horsel here the air is hot;
Right little peace one hath for it, God wot;
   The scented dusty daylight burns the air,
And my heart chokes me till I hear it not.

Behold, my Venus, my soul's body, lies
With my love laid upon her garment-wise,
   Feeling my love in all her limbs and hair
And shed between her eyelids through her eyes.

She holds my heart in her sweet open hands
Hanging asleep; hard by her head there stands,
   Crowned with gilt thorns and clothed with flesh like
      fire,
Love, wan as foam blown up the salt burnt sands—

Hot as the brackish waifs of yellow spume
That shift and steam—loose clots of arid fume
   From the sea's panting mouth of dry desire;
There stands he, like one labouring at a loom.

The warp holds fast across; and every thread
That makes the woof up has dry specks of red;
   Always the shuttle cleaves clean through, and he
Weaves with the hair of many a ruined head.

Love is not glad nor sorry, as I deem;
Labouring he dreams, and labours in the dream,
   Till when the spool is finished, lo I see
His web, reeled off, curls and goes out like steam.

Night falls like fire; the heavy lights run low,
And as they drop, my blood and body so
   Shake as the flame shakes, full of days and hours
That sleep not neither weep they as they go.

[33]

Ah yet would God this flesh of mine might be
Where air might wash and long leaves cover me,
    Where tides of grass break into foam of flowers,
Or where the wind's feet shine along the sea.

Ah yet would God that stems and roots were bred
Out of my weary body and my head,
    That sleep were sealed upon me with a seal,
And I were as the least of all his dead.

Would God my blood were dew to feed the grass,
Mine ears made deaf and mine eyes blind as glass,
    My body broken as a turning wheel,
And my mouth stricken ere it saith Alas!

Ah God, that love were as a flower or flame,
That life were as the naming of a name,
    That death were not more pitiful than desire,
That these things were not one thing and the same!

Behold now, surely somewhere there is death:
For each man hath some space of years, he saith,
    A little space of time ere time expire,
A little day, a little way of breath.

And lo, between the sundawn and the sun,
His day's work and his night's work are undone;
    And lo, between the nightfall and the light,
He is not, and none knoweth of such an one.

Ah God, that I were as all souls that be,
As any herb or leaf of any tree,
    As men that toil through hours of labouring night,
As bones of men under the deep sharp sea.

Outside it must be winter among men;
For at the gold bars of the gates again
   I heard all night and all the hours of it
The wind's wet wings and fingers drip with rain.

Knights gather, riding sharp for cold; I know
The ways and woods are strangled with the snow;
   And with short song the maidens spin and sit
Until Christ's birthnight, lily-like, arow.

The scent and shadow shed about me make
The very soul in all my senses ache;
   The hot hard night is fed upon my breath,
And sleep beholds me from afar awake.

Alas, but surely where the hills grow deep,
Or where the wild ways of the sea are steep,
   Or in strange places somewhere there is death,
And on death's face the scattered hair of sleep.

There lover-like with lips and limbs that meet
They lie, they pluck sweet fruit of life and eat;
   But me the hot and hungry days devour,
And in my mouth no fruit of theirs is sweet.

No fruit of theirs but fruit of my desire,
For her love's sake whose lips through mine respire;
   Her eyelids on her eyes like flower on flower,
Mine eyelids on mine eyes like fire on fire.

So lie we, not as sleep that lies by death,
With heavy kisses and with happy breath;
   Not as man lies by woman, when the bride
Laughs low for love's sake and the words he saith.

For she lies, laughing low with love; she lies
And turns his kisses on her lips to sighs,
   To sighing sound of lips unsatisfied,
And the sweet tears are tender with her eyes.

Ah, not as they, but as the souls that were
Slain in the old time, having found her fair;
   Who, sleeping with her lips upon their eyes,
Heard sudden serpents hiss across her hair.

Their blood runs round the roots of time like rain:
She casts them forth and gathers them again;
   With nerve and bone she weaves and multiplies
Exceeding pleasure out of extreme pain.

Her little chambers drip with flower-like red,
Her girdles, and the chaplets of her head,
   Her armlets and her anklets; with her feet
She tramples all that winepress of the dead.

Her gateways smoke with fume of flowers and fires,
With loves burnt out and unassuaged desires;
   Between her lips the steam of them is sweet,
The languor in her ears of many lyres.

Her beds are full of perfume and sad sound,
Her doors are made with music, and barred round
   With sighing and with laughter and with tears,
With tears whereby strong souls of men are bound.

There is the knight Adonis that was slain;
With flesh and blood she chains him for a chain;
   The body and the spirit in her ears
Cry, for her lips divide him vein by vein.

[36]

Yea, all she slayeth; yea, every man save me;
Me, love, thy lover that must cleave to thee
   Till the ending of the days and ways of earth,
The shaking of the sources of the sea.

Me, most forsaken of all souls that fell;
Me, satiated with things insatiable;
   Me, for whose sake the extreme hell makes mirth,
Yea, laughter kindles at the heart of hell.

Alas thy beauty! for thy mouth's sweet sake
My soul is bitter to me, my limbs quake
   As water, as the flesh of men that weep,
As their heart's vein whose heart goes nigh to break.

Ah God, that sleep with flower-sweet finger-tips
Would crush the fruit of death upon my lips;
   Ah God, that death would tread the grapes of sleep
And wring their juice upon me as it drips.

There is no change of cheer for many days,
But change of chimes high up in the air, that sways
   Rung by the running fingers of the wind;
And singing sorrows heard on hidden ways.

Day smiteth day in twain, night sundereth night,
And on mine eyes the dark sits as the light;
   Yea, Lord, thou knowest I know not, having sinned,
If heaven be clean or unclean in thy sight.

Yea, as if earth were sprinkled over me,
Such chafed harsh earth as chokes a sandy sea,
   Each pore doth yearn, and the dried blood thereof
Gasps by sick fits, my heart swims heavily,

There is a feverish famine in my veins;
Below her bosom, where a crushed grape stains
   The white and blue, there my lips caught and clove
An hour since, and what mark of me remains?

I dare not always touch her, lest the kiss
Leave my lips charred. Yea, Lord, a little bliss,
   Brief bitter bliss, one hath for a great sin;
Nathless thou knowest how sweet a thing it is.

Sin, is it sin whereby men's souls are thrust
Into the pit? yet had I a good trust
   To save my soul before it slipped therein,
Trod under by the fire-shod feet of lust.

For if mine eyes fail and my soul takes breath,
I look between the iron sides of death
   Into sad hell where all sweet love hath end,
All but the pain that never finisheth.

There are the naked faces of great kings,
The singing folk with all their lute-playings;
   There when one cometh he shall have to friend
The grave that covets and the worm that clings.

There sit the knights that were so great of hand,
The ladies that were queens of fair green land,
   Grown grey and black now, brought unto the dust,
Soiled, without raiment, clad about with sand.

There is one end for all of them; they sit
Naked and sad, they drink the dregs of it,
   Trodden as grapes in the wine-press of lust,
Trampled and trodden by the fiery feet.

I see the marvellous mouth whereby there fell
Cities and people whom the gods loved well,
　　Yet for her sake on them the fire gat hold,
And for their sakes on her the fire of hell.

And softer than the Egyptian lote-leaf is,
The queen whose face was worth the world to kiss,
　　Wearing at breast a suckling snake of gold;
And large pale lips of strong Semiramis,

Curled like a tiger's that curl back to feed;
Red only where the last kiss made them bleed;
　　Her hair most thick with many a carven gem,
Deep in the mane, great-chested, like a steed.

Yea, with red sin the faces of them shine;
But in all these there was no sin like mine;
　　No, not in all the strange great sins of them
That made the wine-press froth and foam with wine.

For I was of Christ's choosing, I God's knight,
No blinkard heathen stumbling for scant light;
　　I can well see, for all the dusty days
Gone past, the clean great time of goodly fight.

I smell the breathing battle sharp with blows,
With shrieks of shafts and snapping short of bows;
　　The fair pure sword smites out in subtle ways,
Sounds and long lights are shed between the rows

Of beautiful mailed men; the edged light slips,
Most like a snake that takes short breath and dips
　　Sharp from the beautifully bending head,
With all its gracious body lithe as lips

That curl in touching you; right in this wise
My sword doth, seeming fire in mine own eyes,
    Leaving all colours in them brown and red
And flecked with death; then the keen breaths like sighs,

The caught-up choked dry laughters following them,
When all the fighting face is grown a flame
    For pleasure, and the pulse that stuns the ears,
And the heart's gladness of the goodly game.

Let me think yet a little; I do know
These things were sweet, but sweet such years ago,
    Their savour is all turned now into tears;
Yea, ten years since, where the blue ripples blow,

The blue curled eddies of the blowing Rhine,
I felt the sharp wind shaking grass and vine
    Touch my blood too, and sting me with delight
Through all this waste and weary body of mine

That never feels clear air; right gladly then
I rode alone, a great way off my men,
    And heard the chiming bridle smite and smite,
And gave each rhyme thereof some rhyme again,

Till my song shifted to that iron one;
Seeing there rode up between me and the sun
    Some certain of my foe's men, for his three
White wolves across their painted coats did run.

The first red-bearded, with square cheeks—alack,
I made my knave's blood turn his beard to black;
    The slaying of him was a joy to see:
Perchance too, when at night he came not back,

Some woman fell a-weeping, whom this thief
Would beat when he had drunken; yet small grief
   Hath any for the ridding of such knaves;
Yea, if one wept, I doubt her teen was brief.

This bitter love is sorrow in all lands,
Draining of eyelids, wringing of drenched hands,
   Sighing of hearts and filling up of graves;
A sign across the head of the world he stands,

As one that hath a plague-mark on his brows;
Dust and spilt blood to track him to his house
   Down under earth; sweet smells of lip and cheek,
Like a sweet snake's breath made more poisonous

With chewing of some perfumed deadly grass,
Are shed all round his passage if he pass,
   And their quenched savour leaves the whole soul weak,
Sick with keen guessing whence the perfume was.

As one who hidden in deep sedge and reeds
Smells the rare scent made where a panther feeds,
   And tracking ever slotwise the warm smell
Is snapped upon by the sweet mouth and bleeds,

His head far down the hot sweet throat of her—
So one tracks love, whose breath is deadlier,
   And lo, one springe and you are fast in hell,
Fast as the gin's grip of a wayfarer.

I think now, as the heavy hours decrease
One after one, and bitter thoughts increase
   One upon one, of all sweet finished things;
The breaking of the battle; the long peace

[41]

Wherein we sat clothed softly, each man's hair
Crowned with green leaves beneath white hoods of vair;
   The sounds of sharp spears at great tourneyings,
And noise of singing in the late sweet air.

I sang of love, too, knowing nought thereof;
'Sweeter,' I said, 'the little laugh of love
   Than tears out of the eyes of Magdalen,
Or any fallen feather of the Dove.

'The broken little laugh that spoils a kiss,
The ache of purple pulses, and the bliss
   Of blinded eyelids that expand again—
Love draws them open with those lips of his,

'Lips that cling hard till the kissed face has grown
Of one same fire and colour with their own;
   Then ere one sleep, appeased with sacrifice,
Where his lips wounded, there his lips atone.'

I sang these things long since and knew them not;
'Lo, here is love, or there is love, God wot,
   This man and that finds favour in his eyes,'
I said, 'but I, what guerdon have I got?

'The dust of praise that is blown everywhere
In all men's faces with the common air;
   The bay-leaf that wants chafing to be sweet
Before they wind it in a singer's hair.'

So that one dawn I rode forth sorrowing;
I had no hope but of some evil thing,
   And so rode slowly past the windy wheat
And past the vineyard and the water-spring,

Up to the Horsel. A great elder-tree
Held back its heaps of flowers to let me see
  The ripe tall grass, and one that walked therein,
Naked, with hair shed over to the knee.

She walked between the blossom and the grass;
I knew the beauty of her, what she was,
  The beauty of her body and her sin,
And in my flesh the sin of hers, alas!

Alas! for sorrow is all the end of this.
O sad kissed mouth, how sorrowful it is!
  O breast whereat some suckling sorrow clings,
Red with the bitter blossom of a kiss!

Ah, with blind lips I felt for you, and found
About my neck your hands and hair enwound,
  The hands that stifle and the hair that stings
I felt them fasten sharply without sound.

Yea, for my sin I had great store of bliss:
Rise up, make answer for me, let thy kiss
  Seal my lips hard from speaking of my sin,
Lest one go mad to hear how sweet it is.

Yet I waxed faint with fume of barren bowers,
And murmuring of the heavy-headed hours;
  And let the dove's beak fret and peck within
My lips in vain, and Love shed fruitless flowers.

So that God looked upon me when your hands
Were hot about me; yea, God brake my bands
  To save my soul alive, and I came forth
Like a man blind and naked in strange lands

That hears men laugh and weep, and knows not whence
Nor wherefore, but is broken in his sense;
    Howbeit I met folk riding from the north
Towards Rome, to purge them of their souls' offence,

And rode with them, and spake to none; the day
Stunned me like lights upon some wizard way,
    And ate like fire mine eyes and mine eyesight;
So rode I, hearing all these chant and pray,

And marvelled; till before us rose and fell
White cursed hills, like outer skirts of hell
    Seen where men's eyes look through the day to night,
Like a jagged shell's lips, harsh, untunable,

Blown in between by devils' wrangling breath;
Nathless we won well past that hell and death,
    Down to the sweet land where all airs are good,
Even unto Rome where God's grace tarrieth.

Then came each man and worshipped at his knees
Who in the Lord God's likeness bears the keys
    To bind or loose, and called on Christ's shed blood,
And so the sweet-souled father gave him ease.

But when I came I fell down at his feet,
Saying, 'Father, though the Lord's blood be right sweet,
    The spot it takes not off the panther's skin,
Nor shall an Ethiop's stain be bleached with it.

'Lo, I have sinned and have spat out at God,
Wherefore his hand is heavier and his rod
    More sharp because of mine exceeding sin,
And all his raiment redder than bright blood

'Before mine eyes; yea, for my sake I wot
The heat of hell is waxen seven times hot
    Through my great sin.' Then spake he some sweet word,
Giving me cheer; which thing availed me not;

Yea, scarce I wist if such indeed were said;
For when I ceased—lo, as one newly dead
    Who hears a great cry out of hell, I heard
The crying of his voice across my head.

'Until this dry shred staff, that hath no whit
Of leaf nor bark, bear blossom and smell sweet,
    Seek thou not any mercy in God's sight,
For so long shalt thou be cast out from it.'

Yea, what if dried-up stems wax red and green,
Shall that thing be which is not nor has been?
    Yea, what if sapless bark wax green and white,
Shall any good fruit grow upon my sin?

Nay, though sweet fruit were plucked of a dry tree,
And though men drew sweet waters of the sea,
    There should not grow sweet leaves on this dead stem,
This waste wan body and shaken soul of me.

Yea, though God search it warily enough,
There is not one sound thing in all thereof;
    Though he search all my veins through, searching them
He shall find nothing whole therein but love.

For I came home right heavy, with small cheer,
And lo my love, mine own soul's heart, more dear
    Than mine own soul, more beautiful than God,
Who hath my being between the hands of her—

Fair still, but fair for no man saving me,
As when she came out of the naked sea
    Making the foam as fire whereon she trod,
And as the inner flower of fire was she.

Yea, she laid hold upon me, and her mouth
Clove unto mine as soul to body doth,
    And, laughing, made her lips luxurious;
Her hair had smells of all the sunburnt south,

Strange spice and flower, strange savour of crushed fruit,
And perfume the swart kings tread underfoot
    For pleasure when their minds wax amorous,
Charred frankincense and grated sandal-root.

And I forgot fear and all weary things,
All ended prayers and perished thanksgivings,
    Feeling her face with all her eager hair
Cleave to me, clinging as a fire that clings

To the body and to the raiment, burning them;
As after death I know that such-like flame
    Shall cleave to me for ever; yea, what care,
Albeit I burn then, having felt the same?

Ah love, there is no better life than this;
To have known love, how bitter a thing it is,
    And afterward be cast out of God's sight;
Yea, these that know not, shall they have such bliss

High up in barren heaven before his face
As we twain in the heavy-hearted place,
    Remembering love and all the dead delight,
And all that time was sweet with for a space?

For till the thunder in the trumpet be,
Soul may divide from body, but not we
    One from another; I hold thee with my hand,
I let mine eyes have all their will of thee,

I seal myself upon thee with my might,
Abiding alway out of all men's sight
    Until God loosen over sea and land
The thunder of the trumpets of the night.

EXPLICIT LAUS VENERIS

Phaedra

Hippolytus; Phædra; Chorus of Trœzenian Women

HIPPOLYTUS

Lay not thine hand upon me; let me go;
Take off thine eyes that put the gods to shame;
What, wilt thou turn my loathing to thy death?

PHÆDRA

Nay, I will never loosen hold nor breathe
Till thou have slain me; godlike for great brows
Thou art, and thewed as gods are, with clear hair:
Draw now thy sword and smite me as thou art god,
For verily I am smitten of other gods,
Why not of thee?

CHORUS

O queen, take heed of words;
Why wilt thou eat the husk of evil speech?
Wear wisdom for that veil about thy head
And goodness for the binding of thy brows.

PHÆDRA

Nay, but this god hath cause enow to smite;
If he will slay me, baring breast and throat,
I lean toward the stroke with silent mouth
And a great heart. Come, take thy sword and slay;
Let me not starve between desire and death,
But send me on my way with glad wet lips;
For in the vein-drawn ashen-coloured palm

Death's hollow hand holds water of sweet draught
To dip and slake dried mouths at, as a deer
Specked red from thorns laps deep and loses pain.
Yea, if mine own blood ran upon my mouth,
I would drink that. Nay, but be swift with me;
Set thy sword here between the girdle and breast,
For I shall grow a poison if I live.
Are not my cheeks as grass, my body pale,
And my breath like a dying poisoned man's?
O whatsoever of godlike names thou be,
By thy chief name I charge thee, thou strong god,
And bid thee slay me. Strike, up to the gold,
Up to the hand-grip of the hilt; strike here;
For I am Cretan of my birth; strike now;
For I am Theseus' wife; stab up to the rims,
I am born daughter to Pasiphae.
See thou spare not for greatness of my blood,
Nor for the shining letters of my name:
Make thy sword sure inside thine hand and smite,
For the bright writing of my name is black,
And I am sick with hating the sweet sun.

HIPPOLYTUS

Let not this woman wail and cleave to me,
That am no part of the gods' wrath with her;
Loose ye her hands from me lest she take hurt.

CHORUS

Lady, this speech and majesty are twain;
Pure shame is of one counsel with the gods.

HIPPOLYTUS

Man is as beast when shame stands off from him.

PHÆDRA

Man, what have I to do with shame or thee?
I am not of one counsel with the gods.
I am their kin, I have strange blood in me,
I am not of their likeness nor of thine:
My veins are mixed, and therefore am I mad,
Yea therefore chafe and turn on mine own flesh,
Half of a woman made with half a god.
But thou wast hewn out of an iron womb
And fed with molten mother-snow for milk.
A sword was nurse of thine; Hippolyta,
That had the spear to father, and the axe
To bridesman, and wet blood of sword-slain men
For wedding-water out of a noble well,
Even she did bear thee, thinking of a sword,
And thou wast made a man mistakingly.
Nay, for I love thee, I will have thy hands,
Nay, for I will not loose thee, thou art sweet,
Thou art my son, I am thy father's wife,
I ache toward thee with a bridal blood,
The pulse is heavy in all my married veins,
My whole face beats, I will feed full of thee,
My body is empty of ease, I will be fed,
I am burnt to the bone with love, thou shalt not go,
I am heartsick, and mine eyelids prick mine eyes,
Thou shalt not sleep nor eat nor say a word
Till thou hast slain me. I am not good to live.

CHORUS

This is an evil born with all its teeth,
When love is cast out of the bound of love.

HIPPOLYTUS

There is no hate that is so hateworthy.

I pray thee turn that hate of thine my way,
I hate not it nor anything of thine.
Lo, maidens, how he burns about the brow,
And draws the chafing sword-strap down his hand.
What wilt thou do? wilt thou be worse than death?
Be but as sweet as is the bitterest,
The most dispiteous out of all the gods,
I am well pleased. Lo, do I crave so much?
I do but bid thee be unmerciful,
Even the one thing thou art. Pity me not:
Thou wert not quick to pity. Think of me
As of a thing thy hounds are keen upon
In the wet woods between the windy ways,
And slay me for a spoil. This body of mine
Is worth a wild beast's fell or hide of hair,
And spotted deeper than a panther's grain.
I were but dead if thou wert pure indeed;
I pray thee by thy cold green holy crown
And by the fillet-leaves of Artemis.
Nay, but thou wilt not. Death is not like thee,
Albeit men hold him worst of all the gods.
For of all gods Death only loves not gifts,
Nor with burnt-offering nor blood-sacrifice
Shalt thou do aught to get thee grace of him;
He will have nought of altar and altar-song,
And from him only of all the lords in heaven
Persuasions turns a sweet averted mouth.
But thou art worse: from thee with baffled breath
Back on my lips my prayer falls like a blow,
And beats upon them, dumb. What shall I say?
There is no word I can compel thee with
To do me good and slay me. But take heed;
I say, be wary; look between thy feet,
Lest a snare take them though the ground be good.

HIPPOLYTUS

Shame may do most where fear is found most weak;
That which for shame's sake yet I have not done,
Shall it be done for fear's? Take thine own way;
Better the foot slip than the whole soul swerve.

PHÆDRA

The man is choice and exquisite of mouth;
Yet in the end a curse shall curdle it.

CHORUS

He goes with cloak upgathered to the lip,
Holding his eye as with some ill in sight.

PHÆDRA

A bitter ill he hath i' the way thereof,
And it shall burn the sight out as with fire.

CHORUS

Speak no such word whereto mischance is kin.

PHÆDRA

Out of my heart and by fate's leave I speak.

CHORUS

Set not thy heart to follow after fate.

PHÆDRA

O women, O sweet people of this land,
O goodly city and pleasant ways thereof,
And woods with pasturing grass and great well-heads,
And hills with light and night between your leaves,
And winds with sound and silence in your lips,
And earth and water and all immortal things,
I take you to my witness what I am.

[52]

There is a god about me like as fire,
Sprung whence, who knoweth, or who hath heart to say?
A god more strong than whom slain beasts can soothe,
Or honey, or any spilth of blood-like wine,
Nor shall one please him with a whitened brow
Nor wheat nor wool nor aught of plaited leaf.
For like my mother am I stung and slain,
And round my cheeks have such red malady
And on my lips such fire and foam as hers.
This is that Atè out of Amathus
That breeds up death and gives it one for love.
She hath slain mercy, and for dead mercy's sake
(Being frighted with this sister that was slain)
Flees from before her fearful-footed shame,
And will not bear the bending of her brows
And long soft arrows flown from under them
As from bows bent. Desire flows out of her
As out of lips doth speech: and over her
Shines fire, and round her and beneath her fire.
She hath sown pain and plague in all our house,
Love loathed of love, and mates unmatchable,
Wild wedlock, and the lusts that bleat or low,
And marriage-fodder snuffed about of kine.
Lo how the heifer runs with leaping flank
Sleek under shaggy and speckled lies of hair,
And chews a horrible lip, and with harsh tongue
Laps alien froth and licks a loathlier mouth.
Alas, a foul first steam of trodden tares,
And fouler of these late grapes underfoot.
A bitter way of waves and clean-cut foam
Over the sad road of sonorous sea
The high gods gave king Theseus for no love,
Nay, but for love, yet to no loving end.
Alas the long thwarts and the fervent oars,
And blown hard sails that straightened the scant rope!

There were no strong pools in the hollow sea
To drag at them and suck down side and beak,
No wind to catch them in the teeth and hair,
No shoal, no shallow among the roaring reefs,
No gulf whereout the straining tides throw spars,
No surf where white bones twist like whirled white fire.
But like to death he came with death, and sought
And slew and spoiled and gat him that he would.
For death, for marriage, and for child-getting,
I set my curse against him as a sword;
Yea, and the severed half thereof I leave
Pittheus, because he slew not (when that face
Was tender, and the life still soft in it)
The small swathed child, but bred him for my fate.
I would I had been the first that took her death
Out from between wet hoofs and reddened teeth,
Splashed horns, fierce fetlocks of the brother bull!
For now shall I take death a deadlier way,
Gathering it up between the feet of love
Or off the knees of murder reaching it.

The Triumph of Time

Before our lives divide for ever,
  While time is with us and hands are free,
(Time, swift to fasten and swift to sever
  Hand from hand, as we stand by the sea)
I will say no word that a man might say
Whose whole life's love goes down in a day;
For this could never have been; and never
  Though the gods and the years relent, shall be.

Is it worth a tear, is it worth an hour,
  To think of things that are well outworn?
Of fruitless husk and fugitive flower,
  The dream foregone and the deed forborne?
Though joy be done with and grief be vain,
Time shall not sever us wholly in twain;
Earth is not spoilt for a single shower;
  But the rain has ruined the ungrown corn.

It will grow not again, this fruit of my heart,
  Smitten with sunbeams, ruined with rain.
The singing seasons divide and depart,
  Winter and summer depart in twain.
It will grow not again, it is ruined at root,
The bloodlike blossom, the dull red fruit;
Though the heart yet sickens, the lips yet smart,
  With sullen savour of poisonous pain.

I have given no man of my fruit to eat;
  I trod the grapes, I have drunken the wine.

Had you eaten and drunken and found it sweet,
This wild new growth of the corn and vine,
This wine and bread without lees or leaven
We had grown as gods, as the gods in heaven,
Souls fair to look upon, goodly to greet,
One splendid spirit, your soul and mine.

In the change of years, in the coil of things,
In the clamour and rumour of life to be,
We, drinking love at the furthest springs,
Covered with love as a covering tree,
We had grown as gods, as the gods above,
Filled from the heart to the lips with love,
Held fast in his hands, clothed warm with his wings,
O love, my love, had you loved but me!

We had stood as the sure stars stand, and moved
As the moon moves, loving the world; and seen
Grief collapse as a thing disproved,
Death consume as a thing unclean.
Twain halves of a perfect heart, made fast
Soul to soul while the years fell past;
Had you loved me once, as you have not loved;
Had the chance been with us that has not been.

I have put my days and dreams out of mind,
Days that are over, dreams that are done.
Though we seek life through, we shall surely find
There is none of them clear to us now, not one.
But clear are these things; the grass and the sand,
Where, sure as the eyes reach, ever at hand,
With lips wide open and face burnt blind,
The strong sea-daisies feast on the sun.

The low downs lean to the sea; the stream,
  One loose thin pulseless tremulous vein,
Rapid and vivid and dumb as a dream,
  Works downward, sick of the sun and the rain;
No wind is rough with the rank rare flowers;
The sweet sea, mother of loves and hours,
Shudders and shines as the grey winds gleam,
  Turning her smile to a fugitive pain.

Mother of loves that are swift to fade,
  Mother of mutable winds and hours.
A barren mother, a mother-maid,
  Cold and clean as her faint salt flowers.
I would we twain were even as she,
Lost in the night and the light of the sea,
Where faint sounds falter and wan beams wade,
  Break, and are broken, and shed into showers.

The loves and hours of the life of a man,
  They are swift and sad, being born of the sea.
Hours that rejoice and regret for a span,
  Born with a man's breath, mortal as he;
Loves that are lost ere they come to birth,
Weeds of the wave, without fruit upon earth.
I lose what I long for, save what I can,
  My love, my love, and no love for me!

It is not much that a man can save
  On the sands of life, in the straits of time,
Who swims in sight of the great third wave
  That never a swimmer shall cross or climb.
Some waif washed up with the strays and spars
That ebb-tide shows to the shore and the stars;
Weed from the water, grass from a grave,
  A broken blossom, a ruined rhyme.

[57]

There will no man do for your sake, I think,
    What I would have done for the least word said.
I had wrung life dry for your lips to drink,
    Broken it up for your daily bread:
Body for body and blood for blood,
As the flow of the full sea risen to flood
That yearns and trembles before it sink,
    I had given, and lain down for you, glad and dead.

Yea, hope at highest and all her fruit,
    And time at fullest and all his dower,
I had given you surely, and life to boot,
    Were we once made one for a single hour.
But now, you are twain, you are cloven apart,
Flesh of his flesh, but heart of my heart;
And deep in one is the bitter root,
    And sweet for one is the lifelong flower.

To have died if you cared I should die for you, clung
    To my life if you bade me, played my part
As it pleased you—these were the thoughts that stung,
    The dreams that smote with a keener dart
Than shafts of love or arrows of death;
These were but as fire is, dust, or breath,
Or poisonous foam on the tender tongue
    Of the little snakes that eat my heart.

I wish we were dead together today,
    Lost sight of, hidden away out of sight,
Clasped and clothed in the cloven clay,
    Out of the world's way, out of the light,
Out of the ages of worldly weather,
Forgotten of all men altogether,
As the world's first dead, taken wholly away,
    Made one with death, filled full of the night.

How we should slumber, how we should sleep,
  Far in the dark with the dreams and the dews!
And dreaming, grow to each other, and weep,
  Laugh low, live softly, murmur and muse;
Yea, and it may be, struck through by the dream,
Feel the dust quicken and quiver, and seem
Alive as of old to the lips, and leap
  Spirit to spirit as lovers use.

Sick dreams and sad of a dull delight;
  For what shall it profit when men are dead
To have dreamed, to have loved with the whole soul's
    might,
  To have looked for day when the day was fled?
Let come what will, there is one thing worth,
To have had fair love in the life upon earth:
To have held love safe till the day grew night,
  While skies had colour and lips were red.

Would I lose you now? would I take you then,
  If I lose you now that my heart has need?
And come what may after death to men,
  What thing worth this will the dead years breed?
Lose life, lose all; but at least I know,
O sweet life's love, having loved you so,
Had I reached you on earth, I should lose not again,
  In death nor life, nor in dream or deed.

Yea, I know this well; were you once sealed mine,
  Mine in the blood's beat, mine in the breath,
Mixed into me as honey in wine,
  Not time, that sayeth and gainsayeth,
Nor all strong things had severed us then;
Not wrath of gods, nor wisdom of men,
Nor all things earthly, nor all divine,
  Nor joy nor sorrow, nor life nor death.

I had grown pure as the dawn and the dew,
　You had grown strong as the sun or the sea.
But none shall triumph a whole life through:
　For death is one, and the fates are three.
At the door of life, by the gate of breath,
There are worse things waiting for men than death;
Death could not sever my soul and you,
　As these have severed your soul from me.

You have chosen and clung to the chance they sent you,
　Life sweet as perfume and pure as prayer.
But will it not one day in heaven repent you?
　Will they solace you wholly, the days that were?
Will you lift up your eyes between sadness and bliss,
Meet mine, and see where the great love is,
And tremble and turn and be changed? Content you;
　The gate is strait; I shall not be there.

But you, had you chosen, had you stretched hand,
　Had you seen good such a thing were done,
I too might have stood with the souls that stand
　In the sun's sight, clothed with the light of the sun;
But who now on earth need care how I live?
Have the high gods anything left to give,
Save dust and laurels and gold and sand?
　Which gifts are goodly; but I will none.

O all fair lovers about the world,
　There is none of you, none, that shall comfort me.
My thoughts are as dead things, wrecked and whirled
　Round and round in a gulf of the sea;
And still, through the sound and the straining stream,
Through the coil and chafe, they gleam in a dream,
The bright fine lips so cruelly curled,
　And strange swift eyes where the soul sits free.

Free, without pity, withheld from woe,
   Ignorant; fair as the eyes are fair.
Would I have you change now, change at a blow
   Startled and stricken, awake and aware?
Yea, if I could, would I have you see
My very love of you filling me,
And know my soul to the quick, as I know
   The likeness and look of your throat and hair?

I shall not change you. Nay, though I might,
   Would I change my sweet one love with a word?
I had rather your hair should change in a night,
   Clear now as the plume of a black bright bird;
Your face fail suddenly, cease, turn grey,
Die as a leaf that dies in a day.
I will keep my soul in a place out of sight,
   Far off, where the pulse of it is not heard.

Far off it walks, in a bleak blown space,
   Full of the sound of the sorrow of years.
I have woven a veil for the weeping face,
   Whose lips have drunken the wine of tears;
I have found a way for the failing feet,
A place for slumber and sorrow to meet;
There is no rumour about the place,
   Nor light, nor any that sees or hears.

I have hidden my soul out of sight, and said
   'Let none take pity upon thee, none
Comfort thy crying: for lo, thou art dead,
   Lie still now, safe out of sight of the sun.
Have I not built thee a grave, and wrought
Thy grave-clothes on thee of grievous thought,
With soft spun verses and tears unshed,
   And sweet light visions of things undone?

'I have given thee garments and balm and myrrh,
  And gold, and beautiful burial things.
But thou, be at peace now, make no stir;
  Is not thy grave as a royal king's?
Fret not thyself though the end were sore;
Sleep, be patient, vex me no more.
Sleep; what hast thou to do with her?
  The eyes that weep, with the mouth that sings?'

Where the dead red leaves of the years lie rotten,
  The cold old crimes and the deeds thrown by,
The misconceived and the misbegotten,
  I would find a sin to do ere I die,
Sure to dissolve and destroy me all through,
That would set you higher in heaven, serve you
And leave you happy, when clean forgotten,
  As a dead man out of mind, am I.

Your lithe hands draw me, your face burns through me,
  I am swift to follow you, keen to see;
But love lacks might to redeem or undo me;
  As I have been, I know I shall surely be;
'What should such fellows as I do?' Nay,
My part were worse if I chose to play;
For the worst is this after all; if they knew me,
  Not a soul upon earth would pity me.

And I play not for pity of these; but you,
  If you saw with your soul what man am I,
You would praise me at least that my soul all through
  Clove to you, loathing the lives that lie;
The souls and lips that are bought and sold,
The smiles of silver and kisses of gold,
The lapdog loves that whine as they chew,
  The little lovers that curse and cry.

[62]

There are fairer women, I hear; that may be;
    But I, that I love you and find you fair,
Who are more than fair in my eyes if they be,
    Do the high gods know or the great gods care?
Though the swords in my heart for one were seven,
Should the iron hollow of doubtful heaven,
That knows not itself whether night-time or day be,
    Reverberate words and a foolish prayer?

I will go back to the great sweet mother,
    Mother and lover of men, the sea.
I will go down to her, I and none other,
    Close with her, kiss her and mix her with me;
Cling to her, strive with her, hold her fast;
O fair white mother, in days long past
Born without sister, born without brother,
    Set free my soul as thy soul is free.

O fair green-girdled mother of mine,
    Sea, that art clothed with the sun and the rain,
Thy sweet hard kisses are strong like wine,
    Thy large embraces are keen like pain.
Save me and hide me with all thy waves,
Find me one grave of thy thousand graves,
Those pure cold populous graves of thine,
    Wrought without hand in a world without stain.

I shall sleep, and move with the moving ships,
    Change as the winds change, veer in the tide;
My lips will feast on the foam of thy lips,
    I shall rise with thy rising, with thee subside;
Sleep, and not know if she be, if she were,
Filled full with life to the eyes and hair,
As a rose is fulfilled to the roseleaf tips
    With splendid summer and perfume and pride.

This woven raiment of nights and days,
  Were it once cast off and unwound from me,
Naked and glad would I walk in thy ways,
  Alive and aware of thy ways and thee;
Clear of the whole world, hidden at home,
Clothed with green and crowned with the foam,
A pulse of the life of thy straits and bays,
  A vein in the heart of the streams of the sea.

Fair mother, fed with the lives of men,
  Thou art subtle and cruel of heart, men say.
Thou hast taken, and shalt not render again;
  Thou art full of thy dead, and cold as they.
But death is the worst that comes of thee;
Thou art fed with our dead, O mother, O sea,
But when hast thou fed on our hearts? or when,
  Having given us love, hast thou taken away?

O tender-hearted, O perfect lover,
  Thy lips are bitter, and sweet thine heart.
The hopes that hurt and the dreams that hover,
  Shall they not vanish away and apart?
But thou, thou art sure, thou art older than earth;
Thou art strong for death and fruitful of birth;
Thy depths conceal and thy gulfs discover;
  From the first thou wert; in the end thou art.

And grief shall endure not for ever, I know.
  As things that are not shall these things be;
We shall live through seasons of sun and of snow,
  And none be grievous as this to me.
We shall hear, as one in a trance that hears,
The sound of time, the rhyme of the years;
Wrecked hope and passionate pain will grow
  As tender things of a spring-tide sea.

Sea-fruit that swings in the waves that hiss,
  Drowned gold and purple and royal rings.
And all time past, was it all for this?
  Times unforgotten, and treasures of things?
Swift years of liking and sweet long laughter,
That wist not well of the years thereafter
Till love woke, smitten at heart by a kiss,
  With lips that trembled and trailing wings?

There lived a singer in France of old
  By the tideless dolorous midland sea.
In a land of sand and ruin and gold
  There shone one woman, and none but she.
And finding life for her love's sake fail,
Being fain to see her, he bade set sail,
Touched land, and saw her as life grew cold,
  And praised God, seeing; and so died he.

Died, praising God for his gift and grace:
  For she bowed down to him weeping, and said
'Live;' and her tears were shed on his face
  Or ever the life in his face was shed.
The sharp tears fell through her hair, and stung
Once, and her close lips touched him and clung
Once, and grew one with his lips for a space;
  And so drew back, and the man was dead.

O brother, the gods were good to you.
  Sleep, and be glad while the world endures.
Be well content as the years wear through
  Give thanks for life, and the loves and lures;
Give thanks for life, O brother, and death,
For the sweet last sound of her feet, her breath,
For gifts she gave you, gracious and few,
  Tears and kisses, that lady of yours.

Rest, and be glad of the gods; but I,
How shall I praise them, or how take rest?
There is not room under all the sky
For me that know not of worst or best,
Dream or desire of the days before,
Sweet things or bitterness, any more.
Love will not come to me now though I die,
As love came close to you, breast to breast.

I shall never be friends again with roses;
I shall loathe sweet tunes, where a note grown strong
Relents and recoils, and climbs and closes,
As a wave of the sea turned back by song.
There are sounds where the soul's delight takes fire,
Face to face with its own desire;
A delight that rebels, a desire that reposes;
I shall hate sweet music my whole life long.

The pulse of war and passion of wonder,
The heavens that murmur, the sounds that shine,
The stars that sing and the loves that thunder,
The music burning at heart like wine,
An armed archangel whose hands raise up
All senses mixed in the spirit's cup
Till flesh and spirit are molten in sunder—
These things are over, and no more mine.

These were a part of the playing I heard
Once, ere my love and my heart were at strife;
Love that sings and hath wings as a bird,
Balm of the wound and heft of the knife.
Fairer than earth is the sea, and sleep
Than overwatching of eyes that weep,
Now time has done with his one sweet word,
The wine and leaven of lovely life.

I shall go my ways, tread out my measure,
    Fill the days of my daily breath
With fugitive things not good to treasure,
    Do as the world doth, say as it saith;
But if we had loved each other—O sweet,
Had you felt, lying under the palms of your feet,
The heart of my heart, beating harder with pleasure
    To feel you tread it to dust and death—

Ah, had I not taken my life up and given
    All that life gives and the years let go,
The wine and honey, the balm and leaven,
    The dreams reared high and the hopes brought low?
Come life, come death, not a word be said;
Should I lose you living, and vex you dead?
I never shall tell you on earth; and in heaven,
    If I cry to you then, will you hear or know?

Les Noyades

Whatever a man of the sons of men
  Shall say to his heart of the lords above,
They have shown man verily, once and again,
  Marvellous mercies and infinite love.

In the wild fifth year of the change of things,
  When France was glorious and blood-red, fair
With dust of battle and deaths of kings,
  A queen of men, with helmeted hair,

Carrier came down to the Loire and slew,
  Till all the ways and the waves waxed red:
Bound and drowned, slaying two by two,
  Maidens and young men, naked and wed.

They brought on a day to his judgement-place
  One rough with labour and red with fight,
And a lady noble by name and face,
  Faultless, a maiden, wonderful, white.

She knew not, being for shame's sake blind,
  If his eyes were hot on her face hard by.
And the judge bade strip and ship them, and bind
  Bosom to bosom, to drown and die.

The white girl winced and whitened; but he
  Caught fire, waxed bright as a great bright flame
Seen with thunder far out on the sea,
  Laughed hard as the glad blood went and came.

Twice his lips quailed with delight, then said,
  'I have but a word to you all, one word;
Bear with me; surely I am but dead;'
  And all they laughed and mocked him and heard.

'Judge, when they open the judgement-roll,
  I will stand upright before God and pray:
"Lord God, have mercy on one man's soul,
  For his mercy was great upon earth, I say.

' "Lord, if I loved thee—Lord, if I served—
  If these who darkened thy fair Son's face
I fought with, sparing not one, nor swerved
  A hand's-breadth, Lord, in the perilous place—

' "I pray thee say to this man, O Lord,
  Sit thou for him at my feet on a throne.
I will face thy wrath, though it bite as a sword,
  And my soul shall burn for his soul, and atone.

' "For, Lord, thou knowest, O God most wise,
  How gracious on earth were his deeds towards me.
Shall this be a small thing in thine eyes,
  That is greater in mine than the whole great sea?"

'I have loved this woman my whole life long,
  And even for love's sake when have I said
"I love you"? when have I done you wrong,
  Living? but now I shall have you dead.

'Yea, now, do I bid you love me, love?
  Love me or loathe, we are one not twain.
But God be praised in his heaven above
  For this my pleasure and that my pain!

[69]

'For never a man, being mean like me,
   Shall die like me till the whole world dies.
I shall drown with her, laughing for love; and she
   Mix with me, touching me, lips and eyes.

'Shall she not know me and see me all through,
   Me, on whose heart as a worm she trod?
You have given me, God requite it you,
   What man yet never was given of God.'

O sweet one love, O my life's delight,
   Dear, though the days have divided us,
Lost beyond hope, taken far out of sight,
   Not twice in the world shall the gods do thus.

Had it been so hard for my love? but I,
   Though the gods gave all that a god can give,
I had chosen rather the gift to die,
   Cease, and be glad above all that live.

For the Loire would have driven us down to the sea,
   And the sea would have pitched us from shoal to shoal;
And I should have held you, and you held me,
   As flesh holds flesh, and the soul the soul.

Could I change you, help you to love me, sweet,
   Could I give you the love that would sweeten death,
We would yield, go down, locked hands and feet,
   Die, drown together, and breath catch breath;

But you would have felt my soul in a kiss,
   And known that once if I loved you well;
And I would have given my soul for this
   To burn for ever in burning hell.

A Leave-taking

Let us go hence, my songs; she will not hear.
Let us go hence together without fear;
Keep silence now, for singing-time is over,
And over all old things and all things dear.
She loves not you nor me as all we love her.
Yea, though we sang as angels in her ear,
    She would not hear.

Let us rise up and part; she will not know.
Let us go seaward as the great winds go,
Full of blown sand and foam; what help is there?
There is no help, for all these things are so,
And all the world is bitter as a tear.
And how these things are, though ye strove to show,
    She would not know.

Let us go home and hence; she will not weep.
We gave love many dreams and days to keep,
Flowers without scent, and fruits that would not grow,
Saying 'If thou wilt, thrust in thy sickle and reap.'
All is reaped now; no grass is left to mow;
And we that sowed, though all we fell on sleep,
    She would not weep.

Let us go hence and rest; she will not love.
She shall not hear us if we sing hereof,
Nor see love's ways, how sore they are and steep.
Come hence, let be, lie still; it is enough.
Love is a barren sea, bitter and deep;
And though she saw all heaven in flower above,
    She would not love.

Let us give up, go down; she will not care.
Though all the stars made gold of all the air,
And the sea moving saw before it move
One moon-flower making all the foam-flowers fair;
Though all those waves went over us, and drove
Deep down the stifling lips and drowning hair,
    She would not care.

Let us go hence, go hence; she will not see.
Sing all once more together; surely she,
She too, remembering days and words that were,
Will turn a little toward us, sighing; but we,
We are hence, we are gone, as though we had not been
    there.
Nay, and though all men seeing had pity on me,
    She would not see.

Itylus

Swallow, my sister, O sister swallow,
    How can thine heart be full of the spring?
    A thousand summers are over and dead.
What hast thou found in the spring to follow?
    What has thou found in thine heart to sing?
    What wilt thou do when the summer is shed?

O swallow, sister, O fair swift swallow,
    Why wilt thou fly after spring to the south,
    The soft south whither thine heart is set?
Shall not the grief of the old time follow?
    Shall not the song thereof cleave to thy mouth?
    Hast thou forgotten ere I forget?

Sister, my sister, O fleet sweet swallow,
    Thy way is long to the sun and the south;
    But I, fulfilled of my heart's desire,
Shedding my song upon height, upon hollow,
    From tawny body and sweet small mouth
    Feed the heart of the night with fire.

I the nightingale all spring through,
    O swallow, sister, O changing swallow,
    All spring through till the spring be done,
Clothed with the light of the night on the dew,
    Sing, while the hours and the wild birds follow,
    Take flight and follow and find the sun.

Sister, my sister, O soft light swallow,
  Though all things feast in the spring's guest-chamber,
    How hast thou heart to be glad thereof yet?
For where thou fliest I shall not follow,
  Till life forget and death remember,
    Till thou remember and I forget.

Swallow, my sister, O singing swallow,
  I know not how thou hast heart to sing.
    Hast thou the heart? is it all past over?
Thy lord the summer is good to follow,
  And fair the feet of thy lover the spring:
    But what wilt thou say to the spring thy lover?

O swallow, sister, O fleeting swallow,
  My heart in me is a molten ember
    And over my head the waves have met.
But thou wouldst tarry or I would follow,
  Could I forget or thou remember,
    Couldst thou remember and I forget.

O sweet stray sister, O shifting swallow,
  The heart's division divideth us.
    Thy heart is light as a leaf of a tree;
But mine goes forth among sea-gulfs hollow
  To the place of the slaying of Itylus,
    The feast of Daulis, the Thracian sea.

O swallow, sister, O rapid swallow,
  I pray thee sing not a little space.
    Are not the roofs and the lintels wet?
The woven web that was plain to follow,
  The small slain body, the flowerlike face,
    Can I remember if thou forget?

O sister, sister, thy first-begotten!
   The hands that cling and the feet that follow,
     The voice of the child's blood crying yet
Who hath remembered me? who hath forgotten?
   Thou hast forgotten, O summer swallow,
     But the world shall end when I forget.

Anactoria

My life is bitter with thy love; thine eyes
Blind me, thy tresses burn me, thy sharp sighs
Divide my flesh and spirit with soft sound,
And my blood strengthens, and my veins abound.
I pray thee sigh not, speak not, draw not breath;
Let life burn down, and dream it is not death.
I would the sea had hidden us, the fire
(Wilt thou fear that, and fear not my desire?)
Severed the bones that bleach, the flesh that cleaves,
And let our sifted ashes drop like leaves.
I feel thy blood against my blood: my pain
Pains thee, and lips bruise lips, and vein stings vein.
Let fruit be crushed on fruit, let flower on flower,
Breast kindle breast, and either burn one hour.
Why wilt thou follow lesser loves? are thine
Too weak to bear these hands and lips of mine?
I charge thee for my life's sake, O too sweet
To crush love with thy cruel faultless feet,
I charge thee keep thy lips from hers or his,
Sweetest, till theirs be sweeter than my kiss:
Lest I too lure, a swallow for a dove,
Erotion or Erinna to my love.
I would my love could kill thee; I am satiated
With seeing thee live, and fain would have thee dead.
I would earth had thy body as fruit to eat,
And no mouth but some serpent's found thee sweet.
I would find grievous ways to have thee slain,
Intense device, and superflux of pain;
Vex thee with amorous agonies, and shake

Life at thy lips and leave it there to ache;
Strain out thy soul with pangs too soft to kill,
Intolerable interludes, and infinite ill;
Relapse and reluctation of the breath,
Dumb tunes and shuddering semitones of death.
I am weary of all thy words and soft strange ways,
Of all love's fiery nights and all his days,
And all the broken kisses salt as brine
That shuddering lips make moist with waterish wine,
And eyes the bluer for all those hidden hours
That pleasure fills with tears and feeds from flowers,
Fierce at the heart with fire that half comes through,
But all the flowerlike white stained round with blue;
The fervent underlid, and that above
Lifted with laughter or abashed with love;
Thine amorous girdle, full of thee and fair,
And leavings of the lilies in thine hair.
Yea, all sweet words of thine and all thy ways,
And all the fruit of nights and flower of days,
And stinging lips wherein the hot sweet brine
That Love was born of burns and foams like wine,
And eyes insatiable of amorous hours,
Fervent as fire and delicate as flowers,
Coloured like night at heart, but cloven through
Like night with flame, dyed round like night with blue,
Clothed with deep eyelids under and above—
Yea, all thy beauty sickens me with love;
Thy girdle empty of thee and now not fair,
And ruinous lilies in thy languid hair.
Ah, take no thought for Love's sake; shall this be,
And she who loves thy lover not love thee?
Sweet soul, sweet mouth of all that laughs and lives,
Mine is she, very mine; and she forgives.
For I beheld in sleep the light that is
In her high place in Paphos, heard the kiss

Of body and soul that mix with eager tears
And laughter stinging through the eyes and ears;
Saw Love, as burning flame from crown to feet,
Imperishable, upon her storied seat;
Clear eyelids lifted toward the north and south,
A mind of many colours, and a mouth
Of many tunes and kisses; and she bowed,
With all her subtle face laughing aloud,
Bowed down upon me, saying, 'Who doth thee wrong,
Sappho?' but thou—thy body is the song,
Thy mouth the music; thou art more than I,
Though my voice die not till the whole world die;
Though men that hear it madden; though love weep,
Though nature change, though shame be charmed to sleep.
Ah, wilt thou slay me lest I kiss thee dead?
Yet the queen laughed from her sweet heart and said:
'Even she that flies shall follow for thy sake,
And she shall give thee gifts that would not take,
Shall kiss that would not kiss thee' (yea, kiss me)
'When thou wouldst not'—when I would not kiss thee!
Ah, more to me than all men as thou art,
Shall not my songs assuage her at the heart?
Ah, sweet to me as life seems sweet to death,
Why should her wrath fill thee with fearful breath?
Nay, sweet, for is she God alone? hath she
Made earth and all the centuries of the sea,
Taught the sun ways to travel, woven most fine
The moonbeams, shed the starbeams forth as wine,
Bound with her myrtles, beaten with her rods,
The young men and the maidens and the gods?
Have we not lips to love with, eyes for tears,
And summer and flower of women and of years?
Stars for the foot of morning, and for noon
Sunlight, and exaltation of the moon;
Waters that answer waters, fields that wear

Lilies, and languor of the Lesbian air?
Beyond those flying feet of fluttered doves,
Are there not other gods for other loves?
Yea, though she scourge thee, sweetest, for my sake,
Blossom not thorns, and flowers not blood should break.
Ah that my lips were tuneless lips, but pressed
To the bruised blossom of thy scourged white breast!
Ah that my mouth for Muses' milk were fed
On the sweet blood thy sweet small wounds had bled!
That with my tongue I felt them, and could taste
The faint flakes from thy bosom to the waist!
That I could drink thy veins as wine, and eat
Thy breasts like honey! that from face to feet
Thy body were abolished and consumed,
And in my flesh thy very flesh entombed!
Ah, ah, thy beauty! like a beast it bites,
Stings like an adder, like an arrow smites.
Ah sweet, and sweet again, and seven times sweet,
The paces and the pauses of thy feet!
Ah sweeter than all sleep or summer air
The fallen fillets fragrant from thine hair!
Yea, though their alien kisses do me wrong,
Sweeter thy lips than mine with all their song;
Thy shoulders whiter than a fleece of white,
And flower-sweet fingers, good to bruise or bite
As honeycomb of the inmost honey-cells,
With almond-shaped and roseleaf-coloured shells
And blood like purple blossom at the tips
Quivering; and pain made perfect in thy lips
For my sake when I hurt thee; O that I
Durst crush thee out of life with love, and die,
Die of thy pain and my delight, and be
Mixed with thy blood and molten into thee!
Would I not plague thee dying overmuch?
Would I not hurt thee perfectly? not touch

Thy pores of sense with torture, and make bright
Thine eyes with bloodlike tears and grievous light?
Strike pang from pang as note is struck from note,
Catch the sob's middle music in thy throat,
Take thy limbs living, and new-mould with these
A lyre of many faultless agonies?
Feed thee with fever and famine and fine drouth,
With perfect pangs convulse thy perfect mouth,
Make thy life shudder in thee and burn afresh,
And wring thy very spirit through the flesh?
Cruel? but love makes all that love him well
As wise as heaven and crueller than hell.
Me hath love made more bitter toward thee
Than death toward man; but were I made as he
Who hath made all things to break them one by one,
If my feet trod upon the stars and sun
And souls of men as his have alway trod,
God knows I might be crueller than God.
For who shall change with prayers or thanksgivings
The mystery of the cruelty of things?
Or say what God above all gods and years
With offering and blood-sacrifice of tears,
With lamentations from strange lands, from graves
Where the snake pastures, from scarred mouths of slaves,
From prison, and from plunging prows of ships
Through flamelike foam of the sea's closing lips—
With thwartings of strange signs, and wind-blown hair
Of comets, desolating the dim air,
When darkness is made fast with seals and bars,
And fierce reluctance of disastrous stars,
Eclipse, and sound of shaken hills, and wings
Darkening, and blind inexpiable things—
With sorrow of labouring moons, and altering light
And travail of the planets of the night,
And weeping of the weary Pleiads seven,

Feeds the mute melancholy lust of heaven?
Is not his incense bitterness, his meat
Murder? his hidden face and iron feet
Hath not man known, and felt them on their way
Threaten and trample all things and every day?
Hath he not sent us hunger? who hath cursed
Spirit and flesh with longing? filled with thirst
Their lips who cried unto him? who bade exceed
The fervid will, fall short the feeble deed,
Bade sink the spirit and the flesh aspire,
Pain animate the dust of dead desire,
And life yield up her flower to violent fate?
Him would I reach, him smite, him desecrate,
Pierce the cold lips of God with human breath,
And mix his immortality with death.
Why hath he made us? what had all we done
That we should live and loathe the sterile sun,
And with the moon wax paler as she wanes,
And pulse by pulse feel time grow through our veins?
Thee too the years shall cover; thou shalt be
As the rose born of one same blood with thee,
As a song sung, as a word said, and fall
Flower-wise, and be not any more at all,
Nor any memory of thee anywhere;
For never Muse has bound above thine hair
The high Pierian flower whose graft outgrows
All summer kinship of the mortal rose
And colour of deciduous days, nor shed
Reflex and flush of heaven about thine head,
Nor reddened brows made pale by floral grief
With splendid shadow from that lordlier leaf.
Yea, thou shalt be forgotten like spilt wine,
Except these kisses of my lips on thine
Brand them with immortality; but me—
Men shall not see bright fire nor hear the sea,

D   [81]

Nor mix their hearts with music, nor behold
Cast forth of heaven, with feet of awful gold
And plumeless wings that make the bright air blind,
Lightning, with thunder for a hound behind
Hunting through fields unfurrowed and unsown—
But in the light and laughter, in the moan
And music, and in grasp of lip and hand
And shudder of water that makes felt on land
The immeasurable tremor of all the sea,
Memories shall mix and metaphors of me.
Like me shall be the shuddering calm of night,
When all the winds of the world for pure delight
Close lips that quiver and fold up wings that ache;
When nightingales are louder for love's sake,
And leaves tremble like lute-strings or like fire;
Like me the one star swooning with desire
Even at the cold lips of the sleepless moon,
As I at thine; like me the waste white noon,
Burnt through with barren sunlight; and like me
The land-stream and the tide-stream in the sea.
I am sick with time as these with ebb and flow,
And by the yearning in my veins I know
The yearning sound of waters; and mine eyes
Burn as that beamless fire which fills the skies
With troubled stars and travailing things of flame;
And in my heart the grief consuming them
Labours, and in my veins the thirst of these,
And all the summer travail of the trees
And all the winter sickness; and the earth,
Filled full with deadly works of death and birth,
Sore spent with hungry lusts of birth and death,
Has pain like mine in her divided breath;
Her spring of leaves is barren, and her fruit
Ashes; her boughs are burdened, and her root
Fibrous and gnarled with poison; underneath

Serpents have gnawn it through with tortuous teeth
Made sharp upon the bones of all the dead,
And wild birds rend her branches overhead.
These, woven as raiment for his word and thought,
These hath God made, and me as these, and wrought
Song, and hath lit it at my lips; and me
Earth shall not gather though she feed on thee.
As a shed tear shalt thou be shed; but I—
Lo, earth may labour, men live long and die,
Years change and stars, and the high God devise
New things, and old things wane before his eyes
Who wields and wrecks them, being more strong than
    they—
But, having made me, me he shall not slay.
Nor slay nor satiate, like those herds of his
Who laugh and live a little, and their kiss
Contents them, and their loves are swift and sweet,
And sure death grasps and gains them with slow feet,
Love they or hate they, strive or bow their knees—
And all these end; he hath his will of these.
Yea, but albeit he slay me, hating me—
Albeit he hide me in the deep dear sea
And cover me with cool wan foam, and ease
This soul of mine as any soul of these,
And give me water and great sweet waves, and make
The very sea's name lordlier for my sake,
The whole sea sweeter—albeit I die indeed
And hide myself and sleep and no man heed,
Of me the high God hath not all his will.
Blossom of branches, and on each high hill
Clear air and wind, and under in clamorous vales
Fierce noises of the fiery nightingales,
Buds burning in the sudden spring like fire,
The wan washed sand and the waves' vain desire,
Sails seen like blown white flowers at sea, and words

That bring tears swiftest, and long notes of birds
Violently singing till the whole world sings—
I Sappho shall be one with all these things,
With all high things for ever; and my face
Seen once, my songs once heard in a strange place,
Cleave to men's lives, and waste the days thereof
With gladness and much sadness and long love.
Yea, they shall say, earth's womb has borne in vain
New things, and never this best thing again;
Borne days and men, borne fruits and wars and wine,
Seasons and songs, but no song more like mine.
And they shall know me as ye who have known me here,
Last year when I loved Atthis, and this year
When I love thee; and they shall praise me, and say
'She hath all time as all we have our day,
Shall she not live and have her will'—even I?
Yea, though thou diest, I say I shall not die.
For these shall give me of their souls, shall give
Life, and the days and loves wherewith I live,
Shall quicken me with loving, fill with breath,
Save me and serve me, strive for me with death.
Alas, that neither moon nor snow nor dew
Nor all cold things can purge me wholly through,
Assuage me nor allay me nor appease,
Till supreme sleep shall bring me bloodless ease;
Till time wax faint in all his periods;
Till fate undo the bondage of the gods,
And lay, to slake and satiate me all through,
Lotus and Lethe on my lips like dew,
And shed around and over and under me
Thick darkness and the insuperable sea.

In the Orchard
(*Provençal Burden*)

Leave go my hands, let me catch breath and see;
Let the dew-fall drench either side of me;
   Clear apple-leaves are soft upon that moon
Seen sidelong like a blossom in the tree;
   Ah God, ah God, that day should be so soon.

The grass is thick and cool, it lets us lie.
Kissed upon either cheek and either eye,
   I turn to thee as some green afternoon
Turns toward sunset, and is loth to die;
   Ah God, ah God that day should be so soon.

Lie closer, lean your face upon my side,
Feel where the dew fell that has hardly dried,
   Hear how the blood beats that went nigh to swoon;
The pleasure lives there when the sense has died;
   Ah God, ah God, that day should be so soon.

O my fair lord, I charge you leave me this:
Is it not sweeter than a foolish kiss?
   Nay take it then, my flower, my first in June,
My rose, so like a tender mouth it is:
   Ah God, ah God, that day should be so soon.

Love, till dawn sunder night from day with fire,
Dividing my delight and my desire,
   The crescent life and love the plenilune,
Love me though dusk begin and dark retire;
   Ah God, ah God, that day should be so soon.

Ah, my heart fails, my blood draws back; I know,
When life runs over, life is near to go;
  And with the slain of love love's ways are strewn,
And with their blood, if love will have it so;
  Ah God, ah God, that day should be so soon.

Ah, do thy will now; slay me if thou wilt;
There is no building now the walls are built,
  No quarrying now the corner-stone is hewn,
No drinking now the vine's whole blood is spilt;
  Ah God, ah God, that day should be so soon.

Nay, slay me now; nay, for I will be slain;
Pluck thy red pleasure from the teeth of pain,
  Break down thy vine ere yet grape-gatherers prune,
Slay me ere day can slay desire again;
  Ah God, ah God, that day should be so soon.

Yea, with thy sweet lips, with thy sweet sword; yea,
Take life and all, for I will die, I say;
  Love, I gave love, is life a better boon?
For sweet night's sake I will not live till day;
  Ah God, ah God, that day should be so soon.

Nay, I will sleep then only; nay, but go.
Ah sweet, too sweet to me, my sweet, I know
  Love, sleep, and death go to the sweet same tune;
Hold my hair fast, and kiss me through it so.
  Ah God, ah God, that day should be so soon.

The Leper

Nothing is better, I well think,
   Than love; the hidden well-water
Is not so delicate to drink:
   This was well seen of me and her.

I served her in a royal house;
   I served her wine and curious meat.
For will to kiss between her brows
   I had no heart to sleep or eat.

Mere scorn God knows she had of me,
   A poor scribe, nowise great or fair,
Who plucked his clerk's hood back to see
   Her curled-up lips and amorous hair.

I vex my head with thinking this.
   Yea, though God always hated me,
And hates me now that I can kiss
   Her eyes, plait up her hair to see

How she then wore it on the brows,
   Yet am I glad to have her dead
Here in this wretched wattled house
   Where I can kiss her eyes and head.

Nothing is better, I well know
   Than love; no amber in cold sea
Or gathered berries under snow:
   That is well seen of her and me.

Three thoughts I make my pleasure of:
  First I take heart and think of this:
That knights's gold hair she chose to love,
  His mouth she had such will to kiss.

Then I remember that sundawn
  I brought him by a privy way
Out at her lattice, and thereon
  What gracious words she found to say.

(Cold rushes for such little feet—
  Both feet could lie into my hand.
A marvel was it of my sweet
  Her upright body could so stand.)

'Sweet friend, God give you thank and grace;
  Now am I clean and whole of shame,
Nor shall men burn me in the face
  For my sweet fault that scandals them.'

I tell you over word by word.
  She, sitting edgewise on her bed,
Holding her feet, said thus. The third,
  A sweeter thing than these, I said.

God, that makes time and ruins it
  And alters not, abiding God,
Changed with disease her body sweet,
  The body of love wherein she abode.

Love is more sweet and comelier
  Than a dove's throat strained out to sing.
All they spat out and cursed at her
  And cast her forth for a base thing.

[88]

They cursed her, seeing how God had wrought
  This curse to plague her, a curse of his,
Fools were they surely, seeing not
  How sweeter than all sweet she is.

He that had held her by the hair,
  With kissing lips blinding her eyes,
Felt her bright bosom, strained and bare,
  Sigh under him, with short mad cries

Out of her throat and sobbing mouth
  And body broken up with love,
With sweet hot tears his lips were loath
  Her own should taste the savour of,

Yea, he inside whose grasp all night
  Her fervent body leapt or lay,
Stained with sharp kisses red and white,
  Found her a plague to spurn away.

I hid her in this wattled house,
  I served her water and poor bread.
For joy to kiss between her brows
  Time upon time I was nigh dead.

Bread failed; we got but well-water
  And gathered grass with dropping seed.
I had such joy of kissing her,
  I had small care to sleep or feed.

Sometimes when service made me glad
  The sharp tears leapt between my lids,
Falling on her, such joy I had
  To do the service God forbids.

'I pray you let me be at peace,
  Get hence, make room for me to die.'
She said that: her poor lip would cease,
  Put up to mine, and turn to cry.

I said, 'Bethink yourself how love
  Fared in us twain, what either did;
Shall I unclothe my soul thereof?
  That I should do this, God forbid.'

Yea, though God hateth us, he knows
  That hardly in a little thing
Love faileth of the work it does
  Till it grow ripe for gathering.

Six months, and now my sweet is dead
  A trouble takes me; I know not
If all were done well, all well said,
  No word or tender deed forgot.

Too sweet, for the least part in her,
  To have shed life out by fragments; yet,
Could the close mouth catch breath and stir,
  I might see something I forget.

Six months, and I sit still and hold
  In two cold palms her cold two feet.
Her hair, half grey half ruined gold,
  Thrills me and burns me in kissing it.

Love bites and stings me through, to see
  Her keen face made of sunken bones.
Her worn-off eyelids madden me,
  That were shot through with purple once.

She said, 'Be good with me; I grow
   So tired for shame's sake, I shall die
If you say nothing:' even so.
   And she is dead now, and shame put by.

Yea, and the scorn she had of me
   In the old time, doubtless vexed her then.
I never should have kissed her. See
   What fools God's anger makes of men!

She might have loved me a little too,
   Had I been humbler for her sake.
But that new shame could make love new
   She saw not—yet her shame did make.

I took too much upon my love,
   Having for such mean service done
Her beauty and all the ways thereof,
   Her face and all the sweet thereon.

Yea, all this while I tended her,
   I know the old love held fast his part:
I know the old scorn waxed heavier,
   Mixed with sad wonder, in her heart.

It may be all my love went wrong—
   A scribe's work writ awry and blurred,
Scrawled after the blind evensong—
   Spoilt music with no perfect word.

But surely I would fain have done
   All things the best I could. Perchance
Because I failed, came short of one,
   She kept at heart that other man's.

I am grown blind with all these things:
　It may be now she hath in sight
Some better knowledge; still there clings
　The old question. Will not God do right?

A Ballad of Burdens

The burden of fair women. Vain delight,
  And love self-slain in some sweet shameful way,
And sorrowful old age that comes by night
  As a thief comes that has no heart by day,
  And change that finds fair cheeks and leaves them grey,
And weariness that keeps awake for hire,
  And grief that says what pleasure used to say;
This is the end of every man's desire.

The burden of bought kisses. This is sore,
  A burden without fruit in childbearing;
Between the nightfall and the dawn threescore,
  Threescore between the dawn and evening.
  The shuddering in thy lips, the shuddering
In thy sad eyelids tremulous like fire,
  Makes love seem shameful and a wretched thing.
This is the end of every man's desire.

The burden of sweet speeches. Nay, kneel down,
  Cover thy head, and weep; for verily
These market-men that buy thy white and brown
  In the last days shall take no thought for thee.
  In the last days like earth thy face shall be,
Yea, like sea-marsh made thick with brine and mire,
  Sad with sick leavings of the sterile sea.
This is the end of every man's desire.

The burden of long living. Thou shalt fear
  Waking, and sleeping mourn upon thy bed;
And say at night 'Would God the day were here,'
  And say at dawn 'Would God the day were dead.'
  With weary days thou shaft be clothed and fed,
And wear remorse of heart for thine attire,
  Pain for thy girdle and sorrow upon thine head;
This is the end of every man's desire.

The burden of bright colours. Thou shalt see
  Gold tarnished, and the grey above the green;
And as the thing thou seest thy face shall be,
  And no more as the thing beforetime seen.
  And thou shalt say of mercy 'It hath been,'
And living, watch the old lips and loves expire,
  And talking, tears shall take thy breath between;
This is the end of every man's desire.

The burden of sad sayings. In that day
  Thou shalt tell all thy days and hours, and tell
Thy times and ways and words of love, and say
  How one was dear and one desirable,
  And sweet was life to hear and sweet to smell,
But now with lights reverse the old hours retire
  And the last hour is shod with fire from hell.
This is the end of every man's desire.

The burden of four seasons. Rain in spring,
  White rain and wind among the tender trees;
A summer of green sorrows gathering,
  Rank autumn in a mist of miseries,
  With sad face set towards the year, that sees
The charred ash drop out of the dropping pyre,
  And winter wan with many maladies;
This is the end of every man's desire.

The burden of dead faces. Out of sight
  And out of love, beyond the reach of hands,
Changed in the changing of the dark and light,
  They walk and weep about the barren lands
  Where no seed is nor any garner stands,
Where in short breaths the doubtful days respire,
  And time's turned glass lets through the sighing sands;
This is the end of every man's desire.

The burden of much gladness. Life and lust
  Forsake thee, and the face of thy delight;
And underfoot the heavy hour strews dust,
  And overhead strange weathers burn and bite;
  And where the red was, lo the bloodless white,
And where truth was, the likeness of a liar,
  And where day was, the likeness of the night;
This is the end of every man's desire.

L'ENVOY

Princes, and ye whom pleasure quickeneth,
  Heed well this rhyme before your pleasure tire;
For life is sweet, but after life is death.
  This is the end of every man's desire.

Rondel

Kissing her hair I sat against her feet,
Wove and unwove it, wound and found it sweet;
Made fast therewith her hands, drew down her eyes,
Deep as deep flowers and dreamy like dim skies;
With her own tresses bound and found her fair,
    Kissing her hair.

Sleep were no sweeter than her face to me,
Sleep of cold sea-bloom under the cold sea;
What pain could get between my face and hers?
What new sweet thing would love not relish worse?
Unless, perhaps, white death had kissed me there,
    Kissing her hair?

Before Parting

A month or twain to live on honeycomb
Is pleasant; but one tires of scented time,
Cold sweet recurrence of accepted rhyme,
And that strong purple under juice and foam
Where the wine's heart has burst;
Nor feel the latter kisses like the first.

Once yet, this poor one time; I will not pray
Even to change the bitterness of it,
The bitter taste ensuing on the sweet,
To make your tears fall where your soft hair lay
All blurred and heavy in some perfumed wise
Over my face and eyes.

And yet who knows what end the scythèd wheat
Makes of its foolish poppies' mouths of red?
These were not sown, these are not harvested,
They grow a month and are cast under feet
And none has care thereof,
As none has care of a divided love.

I know each shadow of your lips by rote,
Each change of love in eyelids and eyebrows;
The fashion of fair temples tremulous
With tender blood, and colour of your throat;
I know not how love is gone out of this,
Seeing that all was his.

Love's likeness there endures upon all these:
But out of these one shall not gather love.
Day hath not strength nor the night shade enough
To make love whole and fill his lips with ease,
As some bee-builded cell
Feels at filled lips the heavy honey swell.

I know not how this last month leaves your hair
Less full of purple colour and hid spice,
And that luxurious trouble of closed eyes
Is mixed with meaner shadow and waste care;
And love, kissed out by pleasure, seems not yet
Worth patience to regret.

The Sundew

A little marsh-plant, yellow green,
And pricked at lip with tender red.
Tread close, and either way you tread
Some faint black water jets between
Lest you should bruise the curious head.

A live thing maybe; who shall know?
The summer knows and suffers it;
For the cool moss is thick and sweet
Each side, and saves the blossom so
That it lives out the long June heat.

The deep scent of the heather burns
About it; breathless though it be,
Bow down and worship; more than we
Is the least flower whose life returns,
Least weed renascent in the sea.

We are vexed and cumbered in earth's sight
With wants, with many memories;
These see their mother what she is,
Glad-growing, till August leave more bright
The apple-coloured cranberries.

Wind blows and bleaches the strong grass,
Blown all one way to shelter it
From trample of strayed kine, with feet
Felt heavier than the moorhen was,
Strayed up past patches of wild wheat.

You call it sundew: how it grows,
If with its colour it have breath,
If life taste sweet to it, if death
Pain its soft petal, no man knows:
Man has no sight or sense that saith.

My sundew, grown of gentle days,
In these green miles the spring begun
Thy growth ere April had half done
With the soft secret of her ways
Or June made ready for the sun.

O red-lipped mouth of marsh-flower,
I have a secret halved with thee.
The name that is love's name to me
Thou knowest, and the face of her
Who is my festival to see.

The hard sun, as thy petals knew,
Coloured the heavy moss-water:
Thou wert not worth green midsummer
Nor fit to live to August blue,
O sundew, not remembering her.

An Interlude

In the greenest growth of the Maytime,
  I rode where the woods were wet,
Between the dawn and the daytime;
  The spring was glad that we met.

There was something the season wanted,
  Though the ways and the woods smelt sweet;
The breath at your lips that panted,
  The pulse of the grass at your feet.

You came, and the sun came after,
  And the green grew golden above;
And the flag-flowers lightened with laughter,
  And the meadow-sweet shook with love.

Your feet in the full-grown grasses
  Moved soft as a weak wind blows;
You passed me as April passes,
  With face made out of a rose.

By the stream where the stems were slender,
  Your bright foot paused at the sedge;
It might be to watch the tender
  Light leaves in the springtime hedge,

On boughs that the sweet month blanches
  With flowery frost of May:
It might be a bird in the branches,
  It might be a thorn in the way.

I waited to watch you linger
  With foot drawn back from the dew,
Till a sunbeam straight like a finger
  Struck sharp through the leaves at you.

And a bird overhead sang *Follow*,
  And a bird to the right sang *Here*;
And the arch of the leaves was hollow,
  And the meaning of May was clear.

I saw where the sun's hand pointed,
  I knew what the bird's note said;
By the dawn and the dewfall anointed,
  You were queen by the gold on your head.

As the glimpse of a burnt-out ember
  Recalls a regret of the sun,
I remember, forget, and remember
  What Love saw done and undone.

I remember the way we parted,
  The day and the way we met;
You hoped we were both broken-hearted,
  And knew we should both forget.

And May with her world in flower
  Seemed still to murmur and smile
As you murmured and smiled for an hour;
  I saw you turn at the stile.

A hand like a white wood-blossom
  You lifted, and waved, and passed,
With head hung down to the bosom,
  And pale, as it seemed, at last.

And the best and the worst of this is
   That neither is most to blame
If you've forgotten my kisses
   And I've forgotten your name.

Hendecasyllabics

In the month of the long decline of roses
I, beholding the summer dead before me,
Set my face to the sea and journeyed silent,
Gazing eagerly where above the sea-mark
Flame as fierce as the fervid eyes of lions
Half divided the eyelids of the sunset;
Till I heard as it were a noise of waters
Moving tremulous under feet of angels
Multitudinous, out of all the heavens;
Knew the fluttering wind, the fluttered foliage,
Shaken fitfully, full of sound and shadow;
And saw, trodden upon by noiseless angels,
Long mysterious reaches fed with moonlight,
Sweet sad straits in a soft subsiding channel,
Blown about by the lips of winds I knew not,
Winds not born in the north nor any quarter,
Winds not warm with the south nor any sunshine;
Heard between them a voice of exultation,
'Lo, the summer is dead, the sun is faded,
Even like as a leaf the year is withered,
All the fruits of the day from all her branches
Gathered, neither is any left to gather.
All the flowers are dead, the tender blossoms,
All are taken away; the season wasted,
Like an ember among the fallen ashes.
Now with light of the winter days, with moonlight,
Light of snow, and the bitter light of hoarfrost,
We bring flowers that fade not after autumn,
Pale white chaplets and crowns and of latter seasons

Fair false leaves (but the summer leaves were falser),
Woven under the eyes of stars and planets
When low light was upon the windy reaches
Where the flower of foam was blown, a lily
Dropt among the sonorous fruitless furrows
And green fields of the sea that make no pasture:
Since the winter begins, the weeping winter,
All whose flowers are tears, and round his temples
Iron blossom of frost is bound for ever.'

Sapphics

All the night sleep came not upon my eyelids,
Shed not dew, nor shook nor unclosed a feather,
Yet with the lips shut close and with eyes of iron
   Stood and beheld me.

Then to me so lying awake a vision
Came without sleep over the seas and touched me,
Softly touched mine eyelids and lips; and I too,
   Full of the vision,

Saw the white implacable Aphrodite,
Saw the hair unbound and the feet unsandalled
Shine as fire of sunset on western waters;
   Saw the reluctant

Feet, the straining plumes of the doves that drew her,
Looking always, looking with necks reverted,
Back to Lesbos, back to the hills whereunder
   Shone Mitylene;

Heard the flying feet of the Loves behind her
Make a sudden thunder upon the waters,
As the thunder flung from the strong unclosing
   Wings of a great wind.

So the goddess fled from her place, with awful
Sound of feet and thunder of wings around her;
While behind a clamour of singing women
   Severed the twilight.

Ah the singing, ah the delight, the passion!
All the Loves wept, listening; sick with anguish,
Stood the crowned nine Muses about Apollo;
    Fear was upon them,

While the tenth sang wonderful things they knew not.
Ah the tenth, the Lesbian! the nine were silent,
None endured the sound of her song for weeping;
    Laurel by laurel,

Faded all their crowns; but about her forehead,
Round her woven tresses and ashen temples
White as dead snow, paler than grass in summer,
    Ravaged with kisses,

Shone a light of fire as a crown for ever.
Yea, almost the implacable Aphrodite
Paused, and almost wept; such a song was that song.
    Yea, by her name too

Called her, saying, 'Turn to me, O my Sappho;'
Yet she turned her face from the Loves, she saw not
Tears for laughter darken immortal eyelids,
    Heard not about her

Fearful fitful wings of the doves departing,
Saw not how the bosom of Aphrodite
Shook with weeping, saw not her shaken raiment,
    Saw not her hands wrung;

Saw the Lesbians kissing across their smitten
Lutes with lips more sweet than the sound of lute-strings,
Mouth to mouth and hand upon hand, her chosen,
    Fairer than all men;

Only saw the beautiful lips and fingers,
Full of songs and kisses and little whispers,
Full of music; only beheld among them
   Soar, as a bird soars

Newly fledged, her visible song, a marvel,
Made of perfect sound and exceeding passion,
Sweetly shapen, terrible, full of thunders,
   Clothed with the wind's wings.

Then rejoiced she, laughing with love, and scattered
Roses, awful roses of holy blossom;
Then the Loves thronged sadly with hidden faces
   Round Aphrodite,

Then the Muses, stricken at heart, were silent;
Yea, the gods waxed pale; such a song was that song.
All reluctant, all with a fresh repulsion,
   Fled from before her.

All withdrew long since, and the land was barren,
Full of fruitless women and music only.
Now perchance, when winds are assuaged at sunset,
   Lulled at the dewfall,

By the grey sea-side, unassuaged, unheard of,
Unbeloved, unseen in the ebb of twilight,
Ghosts of outcast women return lamenting,
   Purged not in Lethe,

Clothed about with flame and with tears, and singing
Songs that move the heart of the shaken heaven,
Songs that break the heart of the earth with pity,
   Hearing, to hear them.

At Eleusis

Men of Eleusis, ye that with long staves
Sit in the market-houses, and speak words
Made sweet with wisdom as the rare wine is
Thickened with honey; and ye sons of these
Who in the glad thick streets go up and down
For pastime or grave traffic or mere chance;
And all fair women having rings of gold
On hands or hair; and chiefest over these
I name you, daughters of this man the king,
Who dipping deep smooth pitchers of pure brass
Under the bubbled well, till each round lip
Stooped with loose gurgle of waters incoming,
Found me an old sick woman, lamed and lean,
Beside a growth of builded olive-boughs
Whence multiplied thick song of thick-plumed throats—
Also wet tears filled up my hollow hands
By reason of my crying into them—
And pitied me; for as cold water ran
And washed the pitchers full from lip to lip,
So washed both eyes full the strong salt of tears.
And ye put water to my mouth, made sweet
With brown hill-berries; so in time I spoke
And gathered my loose knees from under me.
Moreover in the broad fair halls this month
Have I found space and bountiful abode
To please me. I Demeter speak of this,
Who am the mother and the mate of things:
For as ill men by drugs or singing words
Shut the doors inward of the narrowed womb

Like a lock bolted with round iron through,
Thus I shut up the body and sweet mouth
Of all soft pasture and the tender land,
So that no seed can enter in by it
Though one sow thickly, nor some grain get out
Past the hard clods men cleave and bite with steel
To widen the sealed lips of them for use.
None of you is there in the peopled street
But knows how all the dry-drawn furrows ache
With no green spot made count of in the black:
How the wind finds no comfortable grass
Nor is assuaged with bud nor breath of herbs;
And in hot autumn when ye house the stacks,
All fields are helpless in the sun, all trees
Stand as a man stripped out of all but skin.
Nevertheless ye sick have help to get
By means and stablished ordinance of God;
For God is wiser than a good man is.
But never shall new grass be sweet in earth
Till I get righted of my wound and wrong
By changing counsel of ill-minded Zeus.
For of all other gods is none save me
Clothed with like power to build and break the year.
I make the lesser green begin, when spring
Touches not earth but with one fearful foot;
And as a careful gilder with grave art
Soberly colours and completes the face,
Mouth, chin and all, of some sweet work in stone,
I carve the shapes of grass and tender corn
And colour the ripe edges and long spikes
With the red increase and the grace of gold.
No tradesman in soft wools is cunninger
To kill the secret of the fat white fleece
With stains of blue and purple wrought in it.
Three moons were made and three moons burnt away

While I held journey hither out of Crete
Comfortless, tended by grave Hecate
Whom my wound stung with double iron point;
For all my face was like a cloth wrung out
With close and weeping wrinkles, and both lids
Sodden with salt continuance of tears.
For Hades and the sidelong will of Zeus
And that lame wisdom that has writhen feet,
Cunning, begotten in the bed of Shame,
These three took evil will at me, and made
Such counsel that when time got wing to fly
This Hades out of summer and low fields
Forced the bright body of Persephone:
Out of pure grass, where she lying down, red flowers
Made their sharp little shadows on her sides,
Pale heat, pale colour on pale maiden flesh—
And chill water slid over her reddening feet,
Killing the throbs in their soft blood; and birds,
Perched next her elbow and pecking at her hair,
Stretched their necks more to see her than even to sing.
A sharp thing is it I have need to say;
For Hades holding both white wrists of hers
Unloosed the girdle and with knot by knot
Bound her between his wheels upon the seat,
Bound her pure body, holiest yet and dear
To me and God as always, clothed about
With blossoms loosened as her knees went down,
Let fall as she let go of this and this
By tens and twenties, tumbled to her feet,
White waifs or purple of the pasturage.
Therefore with only going up and down
My feet were wasted, and the gracious air,
To me discomfortable and dun, became
As weak smoke blowing in the under world.
And finding in the process of ill days

What part had Zeus herein, and how as mate
He coped with Hades, yokefellow in sin,
I set my lips against the meat of gods
And drank not neither ate or slept in heaven.
Nor in the golden greeting of their mouths
Did ear take note of me, nor eye at all
Track my feet going in the ways of them.
Like a great fire on some strait slip of land
Between two washing inlets of wet sea
That burns the grass up to each lip of beach
And strengthens, waxing in the growth of wind,
So burnt my soul in me at heaven and earth,
Each way a ruin and a hungry plague,
Visible evil; nor could any night
Put cool between mine eyelids, nor the sun
With competence of gold fill out my want.
Yea so my flame burnt up the grass and stones,
Shone to the salt-white edges of thin sea,
Distempered all the gracious work, and made
Sick change, unseasonable increase of days
And scant avail of seasons; for by this
The fair gods faint in hollow heaven: there comes
No taste of burnings of the twofold fat
To leave their palates smooth, nor in their lips
Soft rings of smoke and weak scent wandering;
All cattle waste and rot, and their ill smell
Grows alway from the lank unsavoury flesh
That no man slays for offering; the sea
And waters moved beneath the heath and corn
Preserve the people of fin-twinkling fish,
And river-flies feed thick upon the smooth;
But all earth over is no man or bird
(Except the sweet race of the kingfisher)
That lacks not and is wearied with much loss.
Meantime the purple inward of the house

Was softened with all grace of scent and sound
In ear and nostril perfecting my praise;
Faint grape-flowers and cloven honey-cake
And the just grain with dues of the shed salt
Made me content: yet my hand loosened not
Its gripe upon your harvest all year long.
While I, thus woman-muffled in wan flesh
And waste externals of a perished face,
Preserved the levels of my wrath and love
Patiently ruled; and with soft offices
Cooled the sharp noons and busied the warm nights
In care of this my choice, this child my choice,
Triptolemus, the king's selected son:
That his fair yearlong body, which hath grown
Strong with strange milk upon the mortal lip
And nerved with half a god, might so increase
Outside the bulk and the bare scope of man:
And waxen over large to hold within
Base breath of yours and this impoverished air,
I might exalt him past the flame of stars,
The limit and walled reach of the great world.
Therefore my breast made common to his mouth
Immortal savours, and the taste whereat
Twice their hard life strains out the coloured veins
And twice its brain confirms the narrow shell.
Also at night, unwinding cloth from cloth
As who unhusks an almond to the white
And pastures curiously the purer taste,
I bared the gracious limbs and the soft feet,
Unswaddled the weak hands, and in mid ash
Laid the sweet flesh of either feeble side,
More tender for impressure of some touch
Than wax to any pen; and lit around
Fire, and made crawl the white worm-shapen flame,
And leap in little angers spark by spark

E   [113]

At head at once and feet; and the faint hair
Hissed with rare sprinkles in the closer curl,
And like scaled oarage of a keen thin fish
In sea-water, so in pure fire his feet
Struck out, and the flame bit not in his flesh,
But like a kiss it curled his lip, and heat
Fluttered his eyelids; so each night I blew
The hot ash red to purge him to full god.
Ill is it when fear hungers in the soul
For painful food, and chokes thereon, being fed;
And ill slant eyes interpret the straight sun,
But in their scope its white is wried to black:
By the queen Metaneira mean I this;
For with sick wrath upon her lips, and heart
Narrowing with fear the spleenful passages,
She thought to thread this web's fine ravel out,
Nor leave her shuttle split in combing it;
Therefore she stole on us, and with hard sight
Peered, and stooped close; then with pale open mouth
As the fire smote her in the eyes between
Cried, and the child's laugh, sharply shortening
As fire doth under rain, fell off; the flame
Writhed once all through and died, and in thick dark
Tears fell from mine on the child's weeping eyes,
Eyes dispossessed of strong inheritance
And mortal fallen anew. Who not the less
From bud of beard to pale-grey flower of hair
Shall wax vinewise to a lordly vine, whose grapes
Bleed the red heavy blood of swoln soft wine,
Subtle with sharp leaves' intricacy, until
Full of white years and blossom of hoary days
I take him perfected; for whose one sake
I am thus gracious to the least who stands
Filleted with white wool and girt upon
As he whose prayer endures upon the lip

And falls not waste: wherefore let sacrifice
Burn and run red in all the wider ways;
Seeing I have sworn by the pale temples' band
And poppied hair of gold Persephone
Sad-tressed and pleached low down about her brows,
And by the sorrow in her lips, and death
Her dumb and mournful-mouthèd minister,
My word for you is eased of its harsh weight
And doubled with soft promise; and your king
Triptolemus, this Celeus dead and swathed
Purple and pale for golden burial,
Shall be your helper in my services,
Dividing earth and reaping fruits thereof
In fields where wait, well-girt, well-wreathen, all
The heavy-handed seasons all year through;
Saving the choice of warm spear-headed share
All beasts that furrow the remeasured land
With their bowed necks of burden equable.

August

There were four apples on the bough,
Half gold half red, that one might know
The blood was ripe inside the core;
The colour of the leaves was more
Like stems of yellow corn that grow
Through all the gold June meadow's floor.

The warm smell of the fruit was good
To feed on, and the split green wood,
With all its bearded lips and stains
Of mosses in the cloven veins,
Most pleasant, if one lay or stood
In sunshine or in happy rains.

There were four apples on the tree,
Red stained through gold, that all might see
The sun went warm from core to rind;
The green leaves made the summer blind
In that soft place they kept for me
With golden apples shut behind.

The leaves caught gold across the sun,
And where the bluest air begun
Thirsted for song to help the heat;
As I to feel my lady's feet
Draw close before the day were done;
Both lips grew dry with dreams of it.

In the mute August afternoon
They trembled to some undertune
Of music in the silver air;
Great pleasure was it to be there
Till green turned duskier and the moon
Coloured the corn-sheaves like gold hair.

That August time it was delight
To watch the red moons wane to white
'Twixt grey seamed stems of apple-trees;
A sense of heavy harmonies
Grew on the growth of patient night,
More sweet than shapen music is.

But some three hours before the moon
The air, still eager from the noon,
Flagged after heat, not wholly dead;
Against the stem I leant my head;
The colour soothed me like a tune,
Green leaves all round the gold and red.

I lay there till the warm smell grew
More sharp, when flecks of yellow dew
Between the round ripe leaves had blurred
The rind with stain and wet; I heard
A wind that blew and breathed and blew,
Too weak to alter its one word.

The wet leaves next the gentle fruit
Felt smoother, and the brown tree-root
Felt the mould warmer: I too felt
(As water feels the slow gold melt
Right through it when the day burns mute)
The peace of time wherein love dwelt.

There were four apples on the tree,
Gold stained on red that all might see
The sweet blood filled them to the core:
The colour of her hair is more
Like stems of fair faint gold, that be
Mown from the harvest's middle floor.

A Christmas Carol*

Three damsels in the queen's chamber,
  The queen's mouth was most fair;
She spake a word of God's mother
  As the combs went in her hair.
    Mary that is of might,
    Bring us to thy Son's sight.

They held the gold combs out from her,
  A span's length off her head;
She sang this song of God's mother
  And of her bearing-bed.
    Mary most full of grace,
    Bring us to thy Son's face.

When she sat at Joseph's hand,
  She looked against her side;
And either way from the short silk band
  Her girdle was all wried.
    Mary that all good may,
    Bring us to thy Son's way.

Mary had three women for her bed,
  The twain were maidens clean;
The first of them had white and red,
  The third had riven green.
    Mary that is so sweet,
    Bring us to thy Son's feet.

*Suggested by a drawing of Mr. D. G. Rossetti's.

She had three women for her hair,
  Two were gloved soft and shod;
The third had feet and fingers bare,
  She was the likest God.
    Mary that wieldeth land,
    Bring us to thy Son's hand.

She had three women for her ease,
  The twain were good women:
The first two were the two Maries,
  The third was Magdalen.
    Mary that perfect is,
    Bring us to thy Son's kiss.

Joseph had three workmen in his stall,
  To serve him well upon;
The first of them were Peter and Paul,
  The third of them was John.
    Mary, God's handmaiden,
    Bring us to thy Son's ken.

'If your child be none other man's,
  But if it be very mine,
The bedstead shall be gold two spans,
  The bedfoot silver fine.'
    Mary that made God mirth,
    Bring us to thy Son's birth.

'If the child be some other man's,
  And if it be none of mine,
The manger shall be straw two spans,
  Betwixen kine and kine.'
    Mary that made sin cease,
    Bring us to thy Son's peace.

Christ was born upon this wise,
    It fell on such a night,
Neither with sounds of psalteries,
    Nor with fire for light.
        Mary that is God's spouse,
        Bring us to thy Son's house.

The star came out upon the east
    With a great sound and sweet:
Kings gave gold to make him feast
    And myrrh for him to eat.
        Mary, of thy sweet mood,
        Bring us to thy Son's good.

He had two handmaids at his head,
    One handmaid at his feet;
The twain of them were fair and red
    The third one was right sweet.
        Mary that is most wise,
        Bring us to thy Son's eyes.
                        Amen.

The Masque of Queen Bersabe
(A Miracle-play)

KING DAVID

Knights mine, all that be in hall,
I have a counsel to you all,
Because of this thing God lets fall
    Among us for a sign.
For some days hence as I did eat
From kingly dishes my good meat,
There flew a bird between my feet
    As red as any wine.
This bird had a long bill of red
And a gold ring above his head;
Long time he sat and nothing said,
Put softly down his neck and fed
    From the gilt patens fine:
And as I marvelled, at the last
He shut his two keen eyën fast
And suddenly woxe big and brast
    Ere one should tell to nine.

PRIMUS MILES

Sir, note this that I will say;
That Lord who maketh corn with hay
And morrows each of yesterday,
    He hath you in his hand.

SECUNDUS MILES (*Paganus quidam*)

By Satan I hold no such thing;
For I wine swell within a king

Whose ears for drink are hot and ring,
The same shall dream of wine-bibbing
    Whilst he can lie or stand.

QUEEN BERSABE

Peace now, lords, for Godis head.
Ye chirk as starlings that be fed
And gape as fishes newly dead;
The devil put your bones to bed,
    Lo, this is all to say.

SECUNDUS MILES

By Mahound, lords, I have good will
This devil's bird to wring and spill;
For now meseems our game goes ill,
    Ye have scant hearts to play.

TERTIUS MILES

Lo, sirs, this word is there said,
That Urias the knight is dead
Through some ill craft; by Poulis head,
I doubt his blood hath made so red
This bird that flew from the queen's bed
    Whereof ye have such fear.

KING DAVID

Yea, my good knave, and is it said
That I can raise men from the dead?
By God I think to have his head
Who saith words of my lady's bed
    For any thief to hear.
  Et percutiat eum in capite.

QUEEN BERSABE

I wis men shall spit at me,
And say, it were but right for thee
That one should hang thee on a tree;
Ho! it were a fair thing to see
The big stones bruise her false body;
    Fie! who shall see her dead?

KING DAVID

I rede you have no fear of this,
For, as ye wot, the first good kiss
I had must be the last of his;
Now are ye queen of mine, I wis,
And lady of a house that is
    Full rich of meat and bread.

PRIMUS MILES

I bid you make good cheer to be
So fair a queen as all men see.
And hold us for your lieges free;
By Peter's soul that hath the key,
    Ye have good hap of it.

SECUNDUS MILES

I would that he were hanged and dead
Who hath no joy to see your head
With gold about it, barred on red,
    That is so scant of wit.

Tunc dicat NATHAN *propheta*
O king, I have a word to thee;
The child that is in Bersabe
Shall wither without light to see;
This word is come of God by me
    For sin that ye have done.

[124]

Because herein ye did not right,
To take the fair one lamb to smite
That was of Urias the knight;
    Ye wist he had but one.
Full many sheep I wot ye had,
And many women, when ye bade,
To do your will and keep you glad,
And a good crown about your head
    With gold to show thereon.
This Urias had one poor house
With low-barred latoun shot-windows
And scant of corn to fill a mouse;
And rusty basnets for his brows,
    To wear them to the bone.
Yea the roofs also, as men sain,
Were thin to hold against the rain;
Therefore what rushes were there lain
Grew wet withouten foot of men;
The stancheons were all gone in twain
    As sick man's flesh is gone.
Nathless he had great joy to see
The long hair of this Bersabe
Fall round her lap and round her knee
Even to her small soft feet, that be
Shod now with crimson royally
    And covered with clean gold.
Likewise great joy he had to kiss
Her throat, where now the scarlet is
Against her little chin, I wis,
    That then was but cold.
No scarlet then her kirtle had
And little gold about it sprad;
But her red mouth was always glad
To kiss, albeit the eyes were sad
    With love they had to hold.

SECUNDUS MILES

How! old thief, thy wits are lame;
To clip such it is no shame;
I rede you in the devil's name,
Ye come not here to make men game;
By Termagaunt that maketh grame,
    I shall to-bete thine head.
  Hic Diabolus capiat eum.
This knave hath sharp fingers, perfay;
Mahound you thank and keep alway,
And give you good knees to pray;
What man hath no lust to play,
The devil wring his ears, I say;
There is no more but wellaway,
    For now am I dead.

KING DAVID

Certes his mouth is wried and black,
Full little pence be in his sack;
This devil hath him by the back,
    It is no boot to lie.

NATHAN

Sitteth now still and learn of me;
A little while and ye shall see
The face of God's strength presently.
All queens made as this Bersabe,
All that were fair and foul ye be,
    Come hither; it am I.

  Et hic omnes cantabunt.

HERODIAS

I am the queen Herodias.
This headband of my temples was
King Herod's gold band woven me.

This broken dry staff in my hand
Was the queen's staff of a great land
    Betwixen Perse and Samarie.
For that one dancing of my feet,
The fire is come in my green wheat,
    From one sea to the other sea.

AHOLIBAH

I am the queen Aholibah.
My lips kissed dumb the word of *Ah*
    Sighed on strange lips grown sick thereby.
God wrought to me my royal bed;
The inner work thereof was red,
    The outer work was ivory.
My mouth's heat was the heat of flame
For lust towards the kings that came
    With horsemen riding royally.

CLEOPATRA

I am the queen of Ethiope.
Love bade my kissing eyelids ope
    That men beholding might praise love.
My hair was wonderful and curled;
My lips held fast the mouth o' the world
    To spoil the strength and speech thereof.
The latter triumph in my breath
Bowed down the beaten brows of death,
    Ashamed they had not wrath enough.

ABIHAIL

I am the queen of Tyrians.
My hair was glorious for twelve spans,
    That dried to loose dust afterward.
My stature was a strong man's length:
My neck was like a place of strength

Built with white walls, even and hard.
Like the first noise of rain leaves catch
One for another, snatch by snatch,
    Is my praise, hissed against and marred.

AZUBAH

I am the queen of Amorites.
My face was like a place of lights
    With multitudes at festival.
The glory of my gracious brows
Was like God's house made glorious
    With colours upon either wall.
Between my brows and hair there was
A white space like a space of glass
    With golden candles over all.

AHOLAH

I am the queen of Amalek.
There was no tender touch or fleck
    To spoil my body or bared feet.
My words were soft like dulcimers,
And the first sweet of grape-flowers
    Made each side of my bosom sweet.
My raiment was as tender fruit
Whose rind smells sweet of spice-tree root,
    Bruised balm-blossom and budded wheat.

AHINOAM

I am the queen Ahinoam.
Like the throat of a soft slain lamb
    Was my throat, softer veined than his:
My lips were as two grapes the sun
Lays his whole weight of heat upon
    Like a mouth heavy with a kiss:
My hair's pure purple a wrought fleece,

My temples therein as a piece
  Of a pomegranate's cleaving is.

ATARAH

I am the queen Sidonian.
My face made faint the face of man,
  And strength was bound between my brows.
Spikenard was hidden in my ships,
Honey and wheat and myrrh in strips,
  White wools that shine as colour does,
Soft linen dyed upon the fold,
Split spice and cores of scented gold,
  Cedar and broken calamus.

SEMIRAMIS

I am the queen Semiramis.
The whole world and the sea that is
  In fashion like a chrysopras,
The noise of all men labouring,
The priest's mouth tired through thanksgiving,
  The sound of love in the blood's pause,
The strength of love in the blood's beat,
All these were cast beneath my feet
  And all found lesser than I was.

HESIONE

I am the queen Hesione.
The seasons that increased in me
  Made my face fairer than all men's.
I had the summer in my hair;
And all the pale gold autumn air
  Was as the habit of my sense.
My body was as fire that shone;
God's beauty that makes all things one
  Was one among my handmaidens.

[129]

CHRYSOTHEMIS

I am the queen of Samothrace.
God, making roses, made my face
    As a rose filled up full with red.
My prows made sharp the straitened seas
From Pontus to that Chersonese
    Whereon the ebbed Asian stream is shed.
My hair was as sweet scent that drips;
Love's breath begun about my lips
    Kindled the lips of people dead.

THOMYRIS

I am the queen of Scythians.
My strength was like no strength of man's,
    My face like day, my breast like spring.
My fame was felt in the extreme land
That hath sunshine on the one hand
    And on the other star-shining.
Yea, and the wind there fails of breath;
Yea, and there life is waste like death;
    Yea, and there death is a glad thing.

HARHAS

I am the queen of Anakim.
In the spent years whose speech is dim,
    Whose raiment is the dust and death,
My stately body without stain
Shone as the shining race of rain
    Whose hair a great wind scattereth.
Now hath God turned my lips to sighs,
Plucked off mine eyelids from mine eyes,
    And sealed with seals my way of breath.

MYRRHA

I am the queen Arabian.

The tears wherewith mine eyelids ran
  Smelt like my perfumed eyelids' smell.
A harsh thirst made my soft mouth hard,
That ached with kisses afterward;
  My brain rang like a beaten bell.
As tears on eyes, as fire on wood,
Sin fed upon my breath and blood,
  Sin made my breasts subside and swell.

PASIPHAE

I am the queen Pasiphae.
Not all the pure clean-coloured sea
  Could cleanse or cool my yearning veins;
Nor any root nor herb that grew,
Flag-leaves that let green water through,
  Nor washing of the dews and rains.
From shame's pressed core I wrung the sweet
Fruit's savour that was death to eat,
  Whereof no seed but death remains.

SAPPHO

I am the queen of Lesbians.
My love, that had no part in man's,
  Was sweeter than all shape of sweet.
The intolerable infinite desire
Made my face pale like faded fire
  When the ashen pyre falls through with heat.
My blood was hot wan wine of love,
And my song's sound the sound thereof,
  The sound of the delight of it.

MESSALINA

I am the queen of Italy.
These were the signs God set on me;
  A barren beauty subtle and sleek,

[131]

Curled carven hair, and cheeks worn wan
With fierce false lips of many a man,
 Large temples where the blood ran weak,
A mouth athirst and amorous
And hungering as the grave's mouth does
 That, being an-hungered, cannot speak.

AMESTRIS

I am the queen of Persians.
My breasts were lordlier than bright swans,
 My body as amber fair and thin.
Strange flesh was given my lips for bread,
With poisonous hours my days were fed,
 And my feet shod with adder-skin.
In Shushan toward Ecbatane
I wrought my joys with tears and pain,
 My loves with blood and bitter sin.

EPHRATH

I am the queen of Rephaim.
God, that some while refraineth him,
 Made in the end a spoil of me.
My rumour was upon the world
As strong sound of swoln water hurled
 Through porches of the straining sea.
My hair was like the flag-flower,
And my breasts carven goodlier
 Than beryl with chalcedony.

PASITHEA

I am the queen of Cypriotes.
Mine oarsmen, labouring with brown throats
 Sang of me many a tender thing.
My maidens, girdled loose and braced
With gold from bosom to white waist,

Praised me between their wool-combing.
All that praise Venus all night long
With lips like speech and lids like song
    Praised me till song lost heart to sing.

ALACIEL

I am the queen Alaciel.
My mouth was like that moist gold cell
    Whereout the thickest honey drips.
Mine eyes were as a grey-green sea;
The amorous blood that smote on me
    Smote to my feet and finger-tips.
My throat was whiter than the dove,
Mine eyelids as the seals of love,
    And as the doors of love my lips.

ERIGONE

I am the queen Erigone.
The wild wine shed as blood on me
    Made my face brighter than a bride's.
My large lips had the old thirst of earth,
Mine arms the might of the old sea's girth
    Bound round the whole world's iron sides.
Within mine eyes and in mine ears
Were music and the wine of tears,
    And light, and thunder of the tides.

Et hic exeant, et dicat Bersabe regina;

Alas, God, for thy great pity
And for the might that is in thee,
Behold, I woful Bersabe
Cry out with stoopings of my knee
And thy wrath laid and bound on me
    Till I may see thy love.
Behold, Lord, this child is grown

[133]

Within me between bone and bone
To make me mother of a son,
Made of my body with strong moan;
There shall not be another one
    That shall be made hereof.

KING DAVID

Lord God, alas, what shall I sain?
Lo, thou art as an hundred men
Both to break and build again:
The wild ways thou makest plain,
Thine hands hold the hail and rain,
And thy fingers both grape and grain;
Of their largess we be all well fain,
    And of their great pity:
The sun thou madest of good gold,
Of clean silver the moon cold,
All the great stars thou hast told
As thy cattle in thy fold
Everyone by his name of old;
Wind and water thou hast in hold,
    Both the land and the long sea;
Both the green sea and the land,
Lord God, thou hast in hand,
Both white water and grey sand;
Upon thy right or thy left hand
There is no man that may stand;
    Lord, thou rue on me.
O wise Lord, if thou be keen
To note things amiss that been,
I am not worth a shell of bean
More than an old mare meagre and lean;
For all my wrong-doing with my queen,
It grew not of our heartes clean,
    But it began of her body.

[134]

For it fell in the hot May
I stood within a paven way
Built of fair bright stone, perfay,
That is as fire of night and day
  And lighteth all my house.
Therein be neither stones nor sticks,
Neither red nor white bricks,
But for cubits five or six
There is most goodly sardonyx
  And amber laid in rows.
It goes round about my roofs,
(If ye list ye shall have proofs)
There is good space for horse and hoofs,
  Plain and nothing perilous.
For the fair green weather's heat,
And for the smell of leavès sweet,
It is no marvel, well ye weet,
  A man to waxen amorous.
This I say now by my case
That spied forth of that royal place;
There I saw in no great space
Mine own sweet, both body and face,
Under the fresh boughs.
In a water that was there
She wesshe her goodly body bare
And dried it with her owen hair:
Both her arms and her knees fair,
  Both bosom and brows;
Both shoulders and eke thighs
Tho she wesshe upon this wise;
Ever she sighed with little sighs,
  And ever she gave God thank.
Yea, God wot I can well see yet
Both her breast and her sides all wet
And her long hair withouten let

[135]

Spread sideways like a drawing net;
Full dear bought and full far fet
Was that sweet thing there y-set;
It were a hard thing to forget
How both lips and eyen met,
 Breast and breath sank.
So goodly a sight as there she was,
Lying looking on her glass
By wan water in green grass,
 Yet saw never man.
So soft and great she was and bright
With all her body waxen white,
I woxe nigh blind to see the light
Shed out of it to left and right;
This bitter sin from that sweet sight
 Between us twain began.

NATHAN

Now, sir, be merry anon,
For ye shall have a full wise son,
Goodly and great of flesh and bone;
There shall no king be such an one,
 I swear by Godis rood.
Therefore, lord, be merry here,
And go to meat withouten fear,
And hear a mass with goodly cheer;
For to all folk ye shall be dear,
 And all folk of your blood.

Et tunc dicant Laudamus.

After Death

The four boards of the coffin lid
Heard all the dead man did.

The first curse was in his mouth,
Made of grave's mould and deadly drouth.

The next curse was in his head,
Made of God's work discomfited.

The next curse was in his hands,
Made out of two grave-bands.

The next curse was in his feet,
Made out of a grave-sheet.

'I had fair coins red and white,
And my name was as great light;

I had fair clothes green and red,
And strong gold bound round my head.

But no meat comes in my mouth,
Now I fare as the worm doth;

And no gold binds in my hair,
Now I fare as the blind fare.

My live thews were of great strength,
Now am I waxen a span's length;

My live sides were full of lust,
Now are they dried with dust.'

The first board spake and said:
'Is it best eating flesh or bread?'

The second answered it:
'Is wine or honey the more sweet?'

The third board spake and said:
'Is red gold worth a girl's gold head?'

The fourth made answer thus:
'All these things are as one with us.'

The dead man asked of them:
'Is the green land stained brown with flame?

Have they hewn my son for beasts to eat,
And my wife's body for beasts' meat?

Have they boiled my maid in a brass pan,
And built a gallows to hang my man?'

The boards said to him:
'This is a lewd thing that ye deem.

Your wife has gotten a golden bed,
All the sheets are sewn with red.

Your son has gotten a coat of silk,
The sleeves are soft as curded milk.

Your maid has gotten a kirtle new,
All the skirt has braids of blue.

Your man has gotten both ring and glove,
Wrought well for eyes to love.'

The dead man answered thus:
'What good gift shall God give us?'

The boards answered him anon:
'Flesh to feed hell's worm upon.'

May Janet
(Breton)

'Stand up, stand up, thou May Janet,
  And go to the wars with me.'
He's drawn her by both hands
  With her face against the sea.

'He that strews red shall gather white,
  He that sows white reap red,
Before your face and my daughter's
  Meet in a marriage-bed.

'Gold coin shall grow in the yellow field,
  Green corn in the green sea-water,
And red fruit grow of the rose's red,
  Ere your fruit grow in her.'

'But I shall have her by land,' he said,
  'Or I shall have her by sea,
Or I shall have her by strong treason
  And no grace go with me.'

Her father's drawn her by both hands,
  He's rent her gown from her,
He's ta'en the smock round her body,
  Cast in the sea-water.

The captain's drawn her by both sides
  Out of the fair green sea;
'Stand up, stand up, thou May Janet,
  And come to the war with me.'

The first town they came to
  There was a blue bride-chamber;
He clothed her on with silk
  And belted her with amber.

The second town they came to
  The bridesmen feasted knee to knee;
He clothed her on with silver,
  A stately thing to see.

The third town they came to
  The bridesmaids all had gowns of gold;
He clothed her on with purple,
  A rich thing to behold.

The last town they came to
  He clothed her white and red,
With green flag either side of her
  And a gold flag overhead.

TRANSLATIONS FROM THE FRENCH
OF VILLON

The complaint of the fair armouress

I

Meseemeth I heard cry and groan
   That sweet who was the armourer's made;
For her young years she made sore moan,
   And right upon this wise she said;
   'Ah fierce old age with foul bald head,
To spoil fair things thou art over fain;
   Who holdeth me? who? would God I were dead!
Would God I were well dead and slain!

II

'Lo, thou hast broken the sweet yoke
   That my high beauty held above
All priests and clerks and merchant-folk;
   There was not one but for my love
   Would give me gold and gold enough,
Though sorrow his very heart had riven,
   To win from me such wage thereof
As now no thief would take if given.

III

'I was right chary of the same,
   God wot it was my great folly,
For love of one sly knave of them,

Good store of that same sweet had he;
　　For all my subtle wiles, perdie,
Got wot I loved him well enow,
　　Right evilly he handled me,
But he loved well my gold, I trow.

IV

'Though I gat bruises green and black,
　　I loved him never the less a jot;
Though he bound burdens on my back,
　　If he said 'Kiss me and heed it not'
　　Right little pain I felt, God wot,
When that foul thief's mouth, found so sweet,
　　Kissed me—much good thereof I got!
I keep the sin and the shame of it.

V

'And he died thirty year agone.
　　I am old now, no sweet thing to see;
By God, though, when I think thereon,
　　And of that good glad time, woe's me,
　　And stare upon my changed body
Stark naked, that has been so sweet,
　　Lean, wizen, like a small dry tree,
I am nigh mad with the pain of it.

VI

'Where is my faultless forehead's white,
　　The lifted eyebrows, soft gold hair,
Eyes wide apart and keen of sight,
　　With subtle skill in the amorous air;
　　The straight nose, great nor small, but fair,
The small carved ears of shapeliest growth,
　　Chin dimpling, colour good to wear,
And sweet red splendid kissing mouth?

[143]

VII

'The shapely slender shoulders small,
　Long arms, hands wrought in glorious wise,
Round little breasts, the hips withal
　High, full of flesh, not scant of size,
Fit for all amorous masteries;
The large loins, and the flower that was
　Planted above my firm round thighs
In a small garden of soft grass?*

VIII

'A writhled forehead, hair gone grey,
　Fallen eyebrows, eyes gone blind and red,
Their laughs and looks all fled away,
　Yea, all that smote men's hearts are fled;
　The bowed nose, fallen from goodlihead;
Foul flapping ears like water-flags;
　Peaked chin, and cheeks all waste and dead.
And lips that are two skinny rags;

IX

'Thus endeth all the beauty of us.
　The arms made short, the hands made lean,
The shoulders bowed and ruinous,
　The breasts, alack! all fallen in;
The flanks too, like the breasts, grown thin;
As for the sweet place, out on it!*
　For the lank thighs, no thighs but skin,
They are specked with spots like sausage-meat.

*See Editor's Note on page 9.

X

'So we make moan for the old sweet days,
  Poor old light women, two or three
Squatting above the straw-fire's blaze,
  The bosom crushed against the knee,
  Like faggots on a heap we be,
Round fires soon lit, soon quenched and done:
  And we were once so sweet, even we!
Thus fareth many and many an one.'

The Epitaph in Form of a Ballad

Which Villon made for Himself and his Comrades,
    Expecting to be Hanged Along with Them

Men, brother men, that after us yet live,
    Let not your hearts too hard against us be;
For if some pity of us poor men ye give,
    The sooner God shall take of you pity.
    Here are we five or six strung up, you see,
And here the flesh that all too well we fed
Bit by bit eaten and rotten, rent and shred,
    And we the bones grow dust and ash withal;
Let no man laugh at us discomforted,
    But pray to God that he forgive us all.

If we call on you, brothers, to forgive,
    Ye should not hold our prayer in scorn, though we
Were slain by law; ye know that all alive
    Have not wit alway to walk righteously;
    Make therefore intercession heartily
With him that of a virgin's womb was bred,
That his grace be not as a dry well-head
    For us, nor let hell's thunder on us fall:
We are dead, let no man harry or vex us dead,
    But pray to God that he forgive us all.

The rain has washed and laundered us all five,
    And the sun dried and blackened; yea perdie,
Ravens and pies with beaks that rend and rive
    Have dug our eyes out, and plucked off for fee

Our beards and eyebrows; never are we free,
Not once, to rest; but here and there still sped,
Drive at its wild will by the wind's change led,
　More pecked of birds than fruits on garden-wall;
Men, for God's love, let no gibe here be said,
　But pray to God that he forgive us all.

Prince Jesus, that of all art Lord and head,
Keep us, that hell be not our bitter bed;
　We have nought to do in such a master's hall.
Be not ye therefore of our fellowhead,
　But pray to God that he forgive us all.

A Lyke-wake Song

Fair of face, full of pride,
Sit ye down by a dead man's side.

Ye sang songs a' the day:
Sit down at night in the red worm's way.

Proud ye were a' day long:
Ye'll be but lean at evensong.

Ye had gowd kells on your hair:
Nae man kens what ye were.

Ye set scorn by the silken stuff:
Now the grave is clean enough.

Ye set scorn by the rubis ring:
Now the worm is a saft sweet thing.

Fine gold and blithe fair face,
Ye are come to a grimly place.

Gold hair and glad grey een.
Nae man kens if ye have been.

An Old Saying

Many waters cannot quench love,
    Neither can the floods drown it.
Who shall snare or slay the white dove
    Faith, whose very dreams crown it,
Gird it round with grace and peace, deep,
Warm, and pure, and soft as sweet sleep?
Many waters cannot quench love,
    Neither can the floods drown it.

Set me as a seal upon thine heart,
    As a seal upon thine arm.
How should we behold the days depart
    And the nights resign their charm?
Love is as the soul: though hate and fear
Waste and overthrow, they strike not here.
Set me as a seal upon thine heart,
    As a seal upon thine arm.

Choruses from

Atalanta in Calydon

A TRAGEDY

When the hounds of spring are on winter's traces

When the hounds of spring are on winter's traces,
   The mother of months in meadow or plain
Fills the shadows and windy places
   With lisp of leaves and ripple of rain;
And the brown bright nightingale amorous
Is half assuaged for Itylus,
For the Thracian ships and the foreign faces,
   The tongueless vigil, and all the pain.

Come with bows bent and with emptying of quivers,
   Maiden most perfect, lady of light,
With a noise of winds and many rivers,
   With a clamour of waters, and with might;
Bind on thy sandals, O thou most fleet,
Over the splendour and speed of thy feet;
For the faint east quickens, the wan west shivers,
   Round the feet of the day and the feet of the night.

Where shall we find her, how shall we sing to her,
   Fold our hands round her knees, and cling?
O that man's heart were as fire and could spring to her,
   Fire, or the strength of the streams that spring!
For the stars and the winds are unto her
As raiment, as songs of the harp-player;
For the risen stars and the fallen cling to her,
   And the southwest-wind and the west-wind sing.

[150]

For winter's rains and ruins are over,
  And all the season of snows and sins;
The days dividing lover and lover,
  The light that loses, the night that wins;
And time remembered is grief forgotten,
And frosts are slain and flowers begotten,
And in green underwood and cover
  Blossom by blossom the spring begins.

The full streams feed on flower of rushes,
  Ripe grasses trammel a travelling foot,
The faint fresh flame of the young year flushes
  From leaf to flower and flower to fruit;
And fruit and leaf are as gold and fire,
And the oat is heard above the lyre,
And the hoofèd heel of a satyr crushes
  The chestnut-husk at the chestnut-root.

And Pan by noon and Bacchus by night,
  Fleeter of foot than the fleet-foot kid,
Follows with dancing and fills with delight
  The Mænad and the Bassarid;
And soft as lips that laugh and hide
The laughing leaves of the trees divide,
And screen from seeing and leave in sight
  The god pursuing, the maiden hid.

The ivy falls with the Bacchanal's hair
  Over her eyebrows hiding her eyes;
The wild vine slipping down leaves bare
  Her bright breast shortening into sighs;
The wild vine slips with the weight of its leaves,
But the berried ivy catches and cleaves
To the limbs that glitter, the feet that scare
  The wolf that follows, the fawn that flies.

Before the beginning of years
   There came to the making of man
Time, with a gift of tears;
   Grief, with a glass that ran;
Pleasure, with pain for leaven;
   Summer, with flowers that fell;
Remembrance fallen from heaven,
   And madness risen from hell;
Strength without hands to smite;
   Love that endures for a breath:
Night, the shadow of light,
   And life, the shadow of death.

And the high gods took in hand
   Fire, and the falling of tears,
And a measure of sliding sand
   From under the feet of the years;
And froth and drift of the sea;
   And dust of the labouring earth;
And bodies of things to be
   In the houses of death and of birth;
And wrought with weeping and laughter,
   And fashioned with loathing and love
With life before and after
   And death beneath and above,
For a day and a night and a morrow,
   That his strength might endure for a span
With travail and heavy sorrow,
   The holy spirit of man.

From the winds of the north and the south
   They gathered as unto strife;
They breathed upon his mouth,
   They filled his body with life;
Eyesight and speech they wrought
   For the veils of the soul therein,
A time for labour and thought,
   A time to serve and to sin;
They gave him light in his ways,
   And love, and a space for delight,
And beauty and length of days,
   And night, and sleep in the night.
His speech is a burning fire;
   With his lips he travaileth;
In his heart is a blind desire,
   In his eyes foreknowledge of death;
He weaves, and is clothed with derision;
   Sows, and he shall not reap;
His life is a watch or a vision
   Between a sleep and a sleep.

We have seen thee, O Love

We have seen thee, O Love, thou art fair; thou art goodly,
   O Love;
Thy wings make light in the air as the wings of a dove.
Thy feet are as winds that divide the stream of the sea;
Earth is thy covering to hide thee, the garment of thee.
Thou art swift and subtle and blind as a flame of fire;
Before thee the laughter, behind thee the tears of desire;
And twain go forth beside thee, a man with a maid;
Her eyes are the eye of a bride whom delight makes
   afraid;
As the breath in the buds that stir is her bridal breath:
But Fate is the name of her; and his name is Death.

For an evil blossom was born
  Of sea-foam and the frothing of blood,
    Blood-red and bitter of fruit,
        And the seed of it laughter and tears,
And the leaves of it madness and scorn;
  A bitter flower from the bud,
    Sprung of the sea without root,
        Sprung without graft from the years.

The weft of the world was untorn
  That is woven of the day on the night,
    The hair of the hours was not white
Nor the raiment of time overworn,
  When a wonder, a world's delight,
  A perilous goddess was born;
    And the waves of the sea as she came
Clove, and the foam at her feet,
    Fawning, rejoiced to bring forth
  A fleshly blossom, a flame
Filling the heavens with heat
      To the cold white ends of the north.

And in air the clamorous birds,
  And men upon earth that hear
Sweet articulate words
    Sweetly divided apart,
  And in shallow and channel and mere
The rapid and footless herds,
    Rejoiced, being foolish of heart.

For all they said upon earth,
  She is fair, she is white like a dove,
    And the life of the world in her breath
Breathes, and is born at her birth;
  For they knew thee for mother of love,
    And knew thee not mother of death.

What hadst thou to do being born,
　　Mother, when winds were at ease,
As a flower of the springtime of corn,
　　A flower of the foam of the seas?
For bitter thou wast from thy birth,
　　Aphrodite, a mother of strife;
For before thee some rest was on earth,
　　A little respite from tears,
　　A little pleasure of life;
For life was not then as thou art,
　　But as one that waxeth in years
Sweet-spoken, a fruitful wife;
　　Earth had no thorn, and desire
No sting, neither death any dart;
　　What hadst thou to do amongst these,
　　Thou, clothed with a burning fire,
Thou, girt with sorrow of heart,
　　Thou, sprung of the seed of the seas
As an ear from a seed of corn,
　　As a brand plucked forth of a pyre,
As a ray shed forth of the morn,
　　For division of soul and disease,
For a dart and a sting and a thorn?
What ailed thee then to be born?

Was there not evil enough,
　　Mother, and anguish on earth
　　Born with a man at his birth,
Wastes underfoot, and above
　　Storm out of heaven, and dearth
Shaken down from the shining thereof,
　　Wrecks from afar overseas
　　And peril of shallow and firth,
　　And tears that spring and increase
In the barren places of mirth,

That thou, having wings as a dove,
Being girt with desire for a girth,
That thou must come after these,
That thou must lay on him love?

Thou shouldst not so have been born:
But death should have risen with thee,
Mother, and visible fear,
Grief, and the wringing of hands,
And noise of many that mourn;
The smitten bosom, the knee
Bowed, and in each man's ear
A cry as of perishing lands,
A moan as of people in prison,
A tumult of infinite griefs;
And thunder of storm on the sands,
And wailing of wives on the shore;
And under these newly arisen
Loud shoals and shipwrecking reefs,
Fierce air and violent light;
Sail rent and sundering oar,
Darkness, and noises of night;
Clashing of streams in the sea,
Wave against wave as a sword,
Clamour of currents, and foam;
Rains making ruin on earth,
Winds that wax ravenous and roam
As wolves in a wolfish horde;
Fruits growing faint in the tree,
And blind things dead in their birth;
Famine, and blighting of corn,
When thy time was come to be born.

All these we know of; but thee
Who shall discern or declare?

In the uttermost ends of the sea
    The light of thine eyelids and hair,
        The light of thy bosom as fire
            Between the wheel of the sun
    And the flying flames of the air?
        Wilt thou turn thee not yet nor have pity,
But abide with despair and desire
    And the crying of armies undone,
        Lamentation of one with another
        And breaking of city by city;
    The dividing of friend against friend,
        The severing of brother and brother;
    Wilt thou utterly bring to an end?
        Have mercy, mother!

For against all men from old
    Thou has set thine hand as a curse,
        And cast out gods from their places.
            These things are spoken of thee.
Strong kings and goodly with gold
    Thou hast found out arrows to pierce,
        And made their kingdoms and races
            As dust and surf of the sea.
All these, overburdened with woes
    And with length of their days waxen weak,
        Thou slewest; and sentest moreover
            Upon Tyro an evil thing,
Rent hair and a fetter and blows
    Making bloody the flower of the cheek,
        Though she lay by a god as a lover,
            Though fair, and the seed of a king.

For of old, being full of thy fire,
    She endured not longer to wear
        On her bosom a saffron vest,

[157]

On her shoulder an ashwood quiver;
Being mixed and made one through desire
With Enipeus, and all her hair
Made moist with his mouth, and her breast
Filled full of the foam of the river.

Who hath given man speech?

Who hath given man speech? or who hath set therein
A thorn for peril and a snare for sin?
For in the word his life is and his breath,
  And in the word his death,
That madness and the infatuate heart may breed
  From the word's womb the deed
And life bring one thing forth ere all pass by,
Even one thing which is ours yet cannot die—
Death. Hast thou seen him ever anywhere,
Time's twin-born brother, imperishable as he
Is perishable and plaintive, clothed with care
  And mutable as sand,
But death is strong and full of blood and fair
And perdurable and like a lord of land?
Nay, time thou seest not, death thou wilt not see
Till life's right hand be loosened from thine hand
  And thy life-days from thee.

For the gods very subtly fashion
  Madness with sadness upon earth:
Not knowing in any wise compassion,
  Nor holding pity of any worth;
And many things they have given and taken,
  And wrought and ruined many things;
The firm land have they loosed and shaken,
  And sealed the sea with all her springs;

They have wearied time with heavy burdens
   And vexed the lips of life with breath:
Set men to labour and given them guerdons,
   Death, and great darkness after death:
Put moans into the bridal measure
   And on the bridal wools a stain;
And circled pain about with pleasure,
   And girdled pleasure about with pain;
And strewed one marriage-bed with tears and fire
For extreme loathing and supreme desire.

What shall be done with all these tears of ours?
   Shall they make watersprings in the fair heaven
To bathe the brows of morning? or like flowers
Be shed and shine before the starriest hours,
   Or made the raiment of the weeping Seven?
Or rather, O our masters, shall they be
Food for the famine of the grievous sea,
   A great well-head of lamentation
Satiating the sad gods? or fall and flow
Among the years and seasons to and fro,
   And wash their feet with tribulation
And fill them full with grieving ere they go?
   Alas, our lords, and yet alas again,
Seeing all your iron heaven is gilt as gold
   But all we smite thereat in vain;
Smite the gates barred with groanings manifold,
   But all the floors are paven with our pain.
Yea, and with weariness of lips and eyes,
With breaking of the bosom, and with sighs,
   We labour, and are clad and fed with grief
And filled with days we would not fain behold
And nights we would not hear of; we wax old,
   All we wax old and wither like a leaf.
We are outcast, strayed between bright sun and moon;

Out light and darkness are as leaves of flowers,
Black flowers and white, that perish; and the noon
　　As midnight, and the night as daylight hours.
　　A little fruit a little while is ours,
　　　　And the worm finds it soon.

But up in heaven the high gods one by one
　　Lay hands upon the draught that quickeneth,
Fulfilled with all tears shed and all things done,
　　And stir with soft imperishable breath
　　The bubbling bitterness of life and death,
And hold it to our lips and laugh; but they
Preserve their lips from tasting night or day,
　　Lest they too change and sleep, the fates that spun,
The lips that made us and the hands that slay;
　　Lest all these change, and heaven bow down to none,
Change and be subject to the secular sway
　　And terrene revolution of the sun.
Therefore they thrust it from them, putting time away.

I would the wine of time, made sharp and sweet
　　With multitudinous days and nights and tears
　　And many mixing savours of strange years,
Were no more trodden of them under feet,
　　Cast out and spilt about their holy places:
That life were given them as a fruit to eat
And death to drink as water; that the light
Might ebb, drawn backward from their eyes, and night
　　Hide for one hour the imperishable faces.
That they might rise up sad in heaven, and know
Sorrow and sleep, one paler than young snow,
　　One cold as blight of dew and ruinous rain;
Rise up and rest and suffer a little, and be
Awhile as all things born with us and we,
　　And grieve as men, and like slain men be slain.

For now we know not of them; but one saith
  The gods are gracious, praising God; and one,
When hast thou seen? or hast thou felt his breath
  Touch, nor consume thine eyelids as the sun,
Nor fill thee to the lips with fiery death?
  None hath beheld him, none
Seen above other gods and shapes of things,
Swift without feet and flying without wings,
Intolerable, not clad with death or life,
  Insatiable, not known of night or day,
The lord of love and loathing and of strife
  Who gives a star and takes a sun away;
Who shapes the soul, and makes her a barren wife
  To the earthly body and grievous growth of clay;
Who turns the large limbs to a little flame
  And binds the great sea with a little sand;
Who makes desire, and slays desire with shame;
  Who shakes the heaven as ashes in his hand;
Who seeks the light and shadow for the same,
  Bids day waste night as fire devours a brand,
Smites without sword, and scourges without rod;
  The supreme evil, God.

Yea, with thine hate, O God, thou hast covered us,
  One saith, and hidden our eyes away from sight,
And made us transitory and hazardous,
  Light things and slight;
Yet have men praised thee, saying, He hath made man
    thus,
  And he doeth right.
Thou hast kissed us, and hast smitten; thou hast laid
Upon us with thy left hand life, and said,
Live: and again thou hast said, Yield up your breath,
And with thy right hand laid upon us death.
Thou hast sent us sleep, and stricken sleep with dreams,

Saying, Joy is not, but love of joy shall be;
Thou hast made sweet springs for all the pleasant streams,
  In the end thou hast made them bitter with the sea.
Thou hast fed one rose with dust of many men;
  Thou hast marred one face with fire of many tears;
Thou hast taken love, and given us sorrow again;
  With pain thou hast filled us full to the eyes and ears.
Therefore because thou art strong, our father, and we
  Feeble; and thou art against us, and thine hand
Constrains us in the shallows of the sea
  And breaks us at the limits of the land;
Because thou hast bent thy lightnings as a bow,
  And loosed the hours like arrows; and let fall
Sins and wild words and many a wingèd woe
  And wars among us, and one end of all;
Because thou hast made the thunder, and thy feet
  Are as a rushing water when the skies
Break, but thy face as an exceeding heat
  And flames of fire the eyelids of thine eyes;
Because thou art over all who are over us;
  Because thy name is life and our name death;
Because thou art cruel and men are piteous,
  And our hands labour and thine hand scattereth;
Lo, with hearts rent and knees made tremulous,
  Lo, with ephemeral lips and casual breath,
    At least we witness of thee ere we die
  That these things are not otherwise, but thus;
  That each man in his heart sigheth, and saith,
    That all men even as I,
All we are against thee, against thee, O God most high.

  But ye, keep ye on earth
  Your lips from over-speech,
Loud words and longing are so little worth;
  And the end is hard to reach.

For silence after grievous things is good,
    And reverence, and the fear that makes men whole,
And shame, and righteous governance of blood,
    And lordship of the soul.
But from sharp words and wits men pluck no fruit,
And gathering thorns they shake the tree at root;
For words divide and rend;
But silence is most noble till the end.

O that I now

O that I now, I too were
By deep wells and water-floods,
Streams of ancient hills, and where
All the wan green places bear
Blossoms cleaving to the sod,
Fruitless fruit, and grasses fair,
Or such darkest ivy-buds
As divide thy yellow hair,
Bacchus, and their leaves that nod
Round they fawnskin brush the bare
Snow-soft shoulders of a god;
There the year is sweet, and there
Earth is full of secret springs,
And the fervent rose-cheeked hours,
Those that marry dawn and noon,
There are sunless, there look pale
In dim leaves and hidden air,
Pale as grass or latter flowers
Or the wild vine's wan wet rings
Full of dew beneath the moon,
And all day the nightingale
Sleeps, and all night sings;
There in cold remote recesses

That nor alien eyes assail,
Feet, nor imminence of wings,
Nor a wind nor any tune,
Thou, O queen and holiest,
Flower the whitest of all things,
With reluctant lengthening tresses
And with sudden splendid breast
Save of maidens unbeholden,
There are wont to enter, there
Thy divine swift limbs and golden
Maiden growth of unbound hair,
Bathed in waters white,
Shine, and many a maid's by thee
In moist woodland or the hilly
Flowerless brakes where wells abound
Out of all men's sight;
Or in lower pools that see
All their marges clothed all round
With the innumerable lily,
Whence the golden-girdled bee
Flits through flowering rush to fret
White or duskier violet,
Fair as those that in far years
With their buds left luminous
And their little leaves made wet,
From the warmer dew of tears,
Mother's tears in extreme need,
Hid the limbs of Iamus,
Of thy brother's seed;
For his heart was piteous
Toward him, even as thine heart now
Pitiful toward us;
Thine, O goddess, turning hither
A benignant blameless brow;
Seeing enough of evil done

And lives withered as leaves wither
In the blasting of the sun;
Seeing enough of hunters dead,
Ruin enough of all our year,
Herds and harvests slain and shed,
Herdsmen stricken many an one,
Fruits and flocks consumed together,
And great length of deadly days.
Yet with reverent lips and fear
Turn we toward thee, turn and praise
For this lightening of clear weather
And prosperities begun.
For not seldom, when all air
As bright water without breath
Shines, and when men fear not, fate
Without thunder unaware
Breaks, and brings down death.
Joy with grief ye great gods give,
Good with bad, and overbear
All the pride of us that live,
All the high estate,
As ye long since overbore,
As in old time long before,
Many a strong man and a great,
All that were.
But do thou, sweet, otherwise,
Having heed of all our prayer,
Taking note of all our sighs;
We beseech thee by thy light,
By thy bow, and thy sweet eyes,
And the kingdom of the night,
Be thou favourable and fair;
By thine arrows and thy might
And Orion overthrown;
By the maiden thy delight,

[165]

By the indissoluble zone
And the sacred hair.

Not as with sundering of the earth

Not as with sundering of the earth
   Nor as with cleaving of the sea
Nor fierce foreshadowings of a birth
   Nor flying dreams of death to be
Nor loosening of the large world's girth
And quickening of the body of night,
   And sound of thunder in men's ears
And fire of lightning in men's sight,
   Fate, mother of desires and fears,
   Bore unto men the law of tears;
But sudden, an unfathered flame,
   And broken out of night, she shone,
She, without body, without name,
   In days forgotten and foregone;
And heaven rang round her as she came
Like smitten cymbals, and lay bare;
   Clouds and great stars, thunders and snows,
The blue sad fields and folds of air,
   The life that breathes, the life that grows,
   All wind, all fire, that burns or blows,
Even all these knew her: for she is great;
   The daughter of doom, the mother of death,
The sister of sorrow; a lifelong weight
   That no man's finger lighteneth,
Nor any god can lighten fate;
A landmark seen across the way
   Where one race treads as the other trod;
An evil sceptre, an evil stay,
   Wrought for a staff, wrought for a rod,
   The bitter jealousy of God.

For death is deep as the sea,
  And fate as the waves thereof.
Shall the waves take pity on thee
  Or the southwind offer thee love?
Wilt thou take the night for thy day
Or the darkness for light on thy way,
  Till thou say in thine heart Enough?
Behold, thou art over fair, thou art over wise;
The sweetness of spring in thine hair, and the light
    in thine eyes.
The light of the spring in thine eyes, and the sound in
  thine ears;
Yet thine heart shall wax heavy with sighs and thine
  eyelids with tears.
Wilt thou cover thine hair with gold, and with silver thy
  feet?
Hast thou taken the purple to fold thee, and made thy
  mouth sweet?
Behold, when thy face is made bare, he that loved thee
  shall hate;
Thy face shall be no more fair at the fall of thy fate.
For thy life shall fall as a leaf and be shed as the rain;
And the veil of thine head shall be grief; and the crown
  shall be pain.

Index of First Lines

[168]